Dramas
with a
Message

VOLUME FIVE

Books by Doug Fagerstrom

Baker Handbook of Single Adult Ministry (gen. ed.)
Counseling Single Adults (gen. ed.)
Dramas with a Message—Volume One
Dramas with a Message—Volume Two
Dramas with a Message—Volume Three
Dramas with a Message—Volume Four
Dramas with a Message—Volume Five
The Lonely Pew (with Jim Carlson)
Single Adult Ministry, the Second Step (gen. ed.)
Single to God (gen. ed.)
Single to Single (gen. ed.)
Singles Ministries Handbook (gen. ed.)
Worship and Drama Library, volume 15

Dramas with a Message

21 Reproducible Dramatic Sketches for the Local Church

VOLUME FIVE

DOUG FAGERSTROM

Kregel Publications

Dramas with a Message: 21 Reproducible Dramatic Sketches for the Local Church—Volume Five

© 2003 by Doug Fagerstrom

Published by Kregel Publications, a division of Kregel, Inc., P.O. Box 2607, Grand Rapids, MI 49501. Kregel Publications provides trusted, biblical publications for Christian growth and service. Your comments and suggestions are valued.

Book design: Kevin Ingram

Library of Congress Cataloging-in-Publication Data
Fagerstrom, Douglas L.
Dramas with a message: 21 reproducible dramatic sketches for the local church—volume five / Doug Fagerstrom.
    p.   cm.
   1. Drama in public worship. 2. Drama in Christian education. 3. Christian drama, American. I. Title.
BV289F34   1999   246'.72—dc21   99-43099
                                              CIP

ISBN 0-8254-2581-6 (v. 1)
ISBN 0-8254-2582-4 (v. 2)
ISBN 0-8254-2583-2 (v. 3)
ISBN 0-8254-2586-7 (v. 4)
ISBN 0-8254-2587-5 (v. 5)

Printed in the United States of America
03 04 05 06 07 / 5 4 3 2 1

A Note to the Drama Director

Dramas with a Message is designed for the worship service or special program in local churches or ministries. Sketches are short—about five to seven minutes in length. Stage setup is simple, often needing only a chair, table, or hand props, and you are permitted to photocopy as many scripts as you need. Actors can be inexperienced, since the characters and lines come out of everyday events.

Some sketches are comical (although that is not their primary purpose), some are serious, and some have an ending that will surprise the audience. All of them carry simple themes. They are not complicated with hidden messages or deep theological truths. While the dramas can stand alone, they often work better as illustrations in a service or program. Not every sketch attempts to deliver an entire message. Some leave the audience "hanging" and in need of a speaker to complete the point. You, the director, will determine how best to fit a sketch into its context.

Know your audience. Know the message for the program. Know your actors. Select the right sketch—and then, have fun! Enjoy the sketches. Build a team of actors and support staff who will value being part of a ministry that delivers biblical principles and truths in an entertaining way.

Blessings as you share the message of Good News through these dramas.

DOUG FAGERSTROM

Acknowledgments

These sketch volumes are dedicated to the faithful actors and actresses at Calvary Church who volunteer their time and talent and have graciously performed these sketches at the "Saturday Night" ministry, each and every week.

Contents

Contents

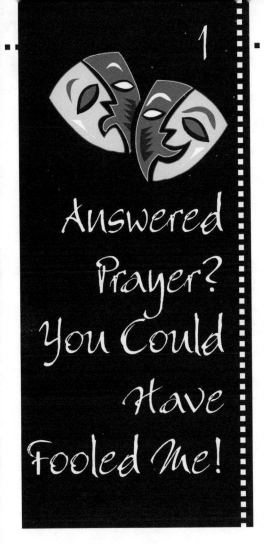

1

Answered Prayer? You Could Have Fooled Me!

THEME

Prayer is often entered into with high expectations that God is going to come through according to our wishes, desires, and demands. God, however, knows what is best. We do not always agree or understand how God is at work in our lives, especially when two believers pray the same prayer and get different results, as we will see in this sketch.

CHARACTERS

BART: A single adult believer in Christ. Nothing seems to go right for Bart.

HERB: Also a single adult believer in Christ. Everything works out right for Herb.

SETTING

Each character is featured in his own "living room." Each side of the platform has a chair or couch, table, phone, lamp, and so forth.

SCENE 1

Both men enter at the same time, walking the same way, sitting down and picking up their Bibles as if they were one person looking in a mirror. They begin to read their Bibles, each very sincere, as they enjoy their quiet time with God. Each freezes while the other speaks.

HERB: *[opening his Bible, and very optimistic]* What a great morning. I wonder what God has for me today?

BART: *[just as positive]* Okay, God, it's You and me again. Go ahead, lay it on me.

BOTH: Ask and it will be given to you,

HERB: . . . seek and you will find;

BART: . . . knock and the door will be opened to you.

BOTH: . . . For everyone who asks receives;

HERB: . . . he who seeks finds,

BART: . . . and to him who knocks,

BOTH: . . . the door will be opened.

BOTH: Wow, that's good stuff. Thanks, God.

HERB: *[excited]* Okay, God, You just said everyone who asks will receive. I need to mention a few things.

BART: *[optimistic]* God, this is great. You said it, I believe it, and . . . that settles it. You and I are going to talk.

HERB: *[sincere]* Lord, the first thing I'd like to mention is my job—you know, I could use that promotion.

BART: Just a few things, God *[pulls out a long list]* Number one, God, . . . the job . . . I'd sure like to get that supervisor's job.

HERB: And, Lord, the station wagon is about shot. . . . A new car would sure be nice in the near future.

BART: Okay, God, . . . next on my little list here is the car. . . . Sure would be nice to get a good deal on a new car. . . . What do you think? Red with bucket seats would be great.

HERB: One more item, Lord. . . . You know my relationship with Rachel . . . well, anything You could do to improve that would be wonderful. . . .

BART: God . . . let me get to the end of this list. . . . Now about my relationship with Ethel . . . I'd really appreciate it if . . . well, You know . . . it sure would be nice if things could come together a little more. . . . Well . . . God, thanks for helping me out on this one.

BOTH: Oh yeah, amen!

[freeze; blackout; exit; music or some type of interlude]

SCENE 2

*Bart enters with hat or briefcase and a stack of mail. He sits in his chair.
Herb enters at the same time and goes to his chair and picks up the phone
to dial. Herb freezes while Bart begins.*

BART: *[going through mail . . . throws a few junk mail pieces on the floor with the following comments]* Sweepstakes Clearing House, ha! Not a chance. . . . You have been preapproved for the three thousand dollars and seven-point-nine percent interest for the next ten days . . . and then twenty-eight percent for the next ten years . . . phone bill, gas bill, the neighbor's mail. . . . Oh great, here's my new car loan. . . . Just what I need. . . . *[opens letter and reads notice]* Dear Mr. Simpson: We are sorry to reject your request for a loan, but the credit report indicates your failure to satisfy this institution's ability to confidently loan you funds at this time . . . REJECT! Ah, here it is, my new job offer. *[opens letter, reads with shock and increasing disbelief]* Dear Mr. Simpson: We regret to inform you that you will be laid off beginning May 1. Please pick up your last paycheck on Friday at the personnel office. *[angry]* Hey, God, what's the deal? You said that whatever I asked for You'd give me. . . . I asked for a promotion . . . not a termination. . . . *[going through mail]* Well, God, that's two for two. Two for You and none for me. *[final letter]* At least I got a good card from Ethel . . . *[cynical toward God, driving home a point . . . very loud]* Since I didn't get any *other* good news today. *[reads card]* Dear Bart: I'm sorry that I haven't called you in the last week. But I need to let you know that I've been seeing someone else over the last three months, and I'm sorry. . . . *[mumbles]* And I'll see you at church this weekend. I'd like you to meet Larry. Your friend, Ethel. *[enraged and extremely cynical]* SORRY! See you at church?! Larry?! Great . . . Hey, God, any more answers to prayer . . . just let me know.

[Phone rings; light comes up on Herb and Bart; Herb breaks freeze]

BART: *[rejected tone]* Bart the loser, who's calling?

HERB: *[looks at the phone]* Bart?

BART: *[extremely cynical]* Mr. good news at your service.

HERB: Bart? This is Herb? Are you okay?

BART: Hey, Herb, I'm just fine. By the way, would you like me to *pray* for you?

HERB: Well, speaking of prayer, I thought I'd give you a call, and since we're in the same Bible study group at the church, I wanted you to know that God has answered some of our prayers.

BART: *[cynicism continues]* Answers to prayers? Great! Go for it, Herb.

HERB: Well, for starters, *[excited]* I got that promotion! You're talking to the vice-president of sales and marketing. . . . And it comes with a *new car.* . . . And, well, last night I popped the big question, and Rachel said *yes.* . . . *[Bart is frozen in a stupor, numb response.]* Bart? Bart? Are you still there?

BART: *[non-emotive]* Yeah, I'm here, Herb, I'm here. *[totally unenthusiastic]* Praise the Lord, Herb. . . .

HERB: *[extremely positive]* That's what I say. Praise the Lord. He does answer prayer! *[freeze]*

BART: *[looking up]* You could have fooled me.

[freeze; blackout]

2

Heaven Bound

THEME

Jesus made it clear—there is only one way to heaven. Many, however, choose to believe that there are many other ways to an eternal destiny with God, as we will see in this sketch.

CHARACTERS

HOWARD: A loud, outgoing, positive, high-energy salesman, convinced that he is going to heaven. He is dressed in a suit, overcoat, and hat, and is carrying a suitcase, obviously ready for a journey.

BOB: An extremely quiet, unassuming individual who doesn't show a lot of emotion, but simply states the facts.

SETTING

At stage center, an outdoor bench and sign that says BUS STOP would be great.

Howard enters very quickly down center aisle carrying a suitcase, ad-libbing* as he greets everyone seated, but obviously does not have time to get a response. Bob enters from back and looks straight ahead, deadpan, no expression. Bob only looks and speaks when spoken to.

HOWARD: *[suggested ad-lib lines* to audience members]* Hi, how are ya. Nice to see ya. Sorry can't talk, I've got to catch the bus . . . don't want to be late. Hey, nice day, isn't it? Gotta run.

HOWARD: *[gregarious, outgoing, trying to be friendly, articulate, and tries to open a conversation with Bob]* Ah . . . hello there, my name is Howard, Howard Bell. And what's your name?

BOB: *[without expression]* Bob.

HOWARD: Hello, Bob, nice to meet you. *[tries to shake hands, no response]* Say, what a beautiful and terrific day, wouldn't you say?

BOB: Sure.

HOWARD: Boy, we haven't had rain for quite some time. . . . Wouldn't want to see those crops go bad. . . . *[makes a drooping ear gesture]* Those little ears of corn need their drink every day, wouldn't you say?

13

BOB: *[beat, pause]* Yup.

HOWARD: *[off to the side]* Real conversationalist, aren't you Bob? *[directly]* Say, I'm headed for heaven. *[chuckles]* Straight ahead, no turning back. . . . You know the song, *[starts singing]* "Heaven is a wonderful place filled with glory and grace, I want to see my Savior's . . ." *[Howard gets stuck; runs through the song again real fast and gets stuck again.]*

BOB: *[Bob fills in the missing word without batting an eye.]* Face!

HOWARD: *[looks at Bob]* Face . . . that's it. Why, thank you, Bob, I appreciate your helping me out. Maybe we could do a little duet together . . . *[resigns to the fact that Bob is not responding]* probably not. Okay. . . . *[awkward, stumbles a little to not embarrass Bob]* Say, you wouldn't by chance be going to . . .

BOB: *[picks up on line]* . . . heaven!

HOWARD: *[excited]* Well, you know, we might be neighbors, Bob!

BOB: *[half smile, monotone]* Whoopee.

HOWARD: *[looking at Bob and then away]* I can see this is going to be a *long* eternity.

BOB: *[kindly, but still no great expression]* How are you planning to get to heaven?

HOWARD: Wait a minute, he talks; he can say more than one word. . . . This must be a miracle. . . . Bob, it's okay, say that again.

BOB: *[repeats identically]* How are you planning to get to heaven?

HOWARD: *[excited]* Tickets, Bob, I have tickets! *[pulls several colored pieces of paper out of his pocket to resemble tickets]* I have so many tickets, I'm going first class. Just call me a member of the frequent flyer club to heaven.

BOB: No thanks.

HOWARD: *[overly enthusiastic]* Look, Bob, *[starts reading off tickets]* I have a ticket for church attendance—twelve consecutive Easters. I have a ticket for tithing—eight percent you know. I have a ticket for volunteerism—City Memorial Day 10 K Run. . . . I handed out ice water. I have a ticket for memorizing the Lord's Prayer. And here, look at this one, sure to get me in with the Big Guy—one ticket to heaven for ushering on Sunday night. Helped those people find their seats. . . . Heaven, here I come! *[looking for Bob's approval]* So, Bob, what do you think?

BOB: Sorry.

HOWARD: Sorry? Sorry about what? *[Howard thinks that Bob is jealous or feeling left out.]* Oh, I see, you don't have any tickets, and you don't think you're going to get into heaven. Okay, Bob, look, I have plenty. How about one of my

tickets, [offers a ticket] and I'll be sure to put in a *good word* for you . . .
seeing as you don't have many for yourself.

BOB: No thanks!

HOWARD: No thanks?! Bob, how in the world do you expect to get to heaven?

BOB: [factually] Jesus.

HOWARD: [wondering] Jesus?

BOB: [confident] Jesus.

HOWARD: Now, Bob, I know you're a man of few words, but you have to do more than just say *Jesus* if you want to go to heaven.

BOB: Nope.

HOWARD: Bob, you need tickets, and to get tickets, you need to be doing things for God. Bob, if you aren't busy earning your ticket to heaven, who do you think is going to pay the price for you to go?

BOB: Jesus!

HOWARD: That's what this has come to, hasn't it, Bob?

BOB: Yup.

HOWARD: Now, let me get this straight, you think that Jesus is the only way to heaven—

BOB: Yup.

HOWARD: [holds out his tickets again] . . . and that all of these tickets are unnecessary.

BOB: Yup.

HOWARD: [beginning to unravel] Bob, this is driving me crazy.

BOB: Good.

HOWARD: So, Mr. Bob-One-Word, Keep-It-Simple Kind-of-Guy, what do you suggest I do to reduce all of these down to Jesus?

BOB: [first real positive expression, as he looks at Howard] Howard, you finally got it.

HOWARD: [pauses to think] Wow.

[freeze; blackout; music plays them off]

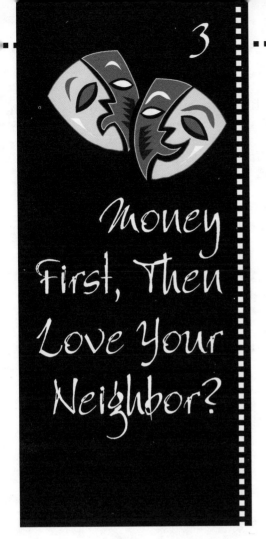

3

Money First, Then Love Your Neighbor?

THEME

"Love your neighbor as yourself" is a direct command from God. But, the question we need to ask is, "Do we?" We often fall short of really loving others. And when we do love others, it's only with our "extras" and "leftovers" as seen in this sad-but-true sketch.

CHARACTERS

VICTORIA: Clearly from the "upper crust" of society with a slight English accent and a nose that is clearly in the air. Her number one priority is Victoria. She is dressed very well.

MARCIA: Our humble "home-girl." She is dressed simply and does not have a very forceful personality. Her family is poor, and she is humiliated to have to make the visit and benevolent request to Victoria.

SETTING

A living room set with a very nice chair, table, lamp, phone, and so forth.

Victoria is on the phone talking to her decorator. Her talk goes back and forth from being syrupy kind to rather nasty.

VICTORIA: Yes, Frederick, I want the flocked wallpaper and the oriental rugs in the entrance way. And be a dear and have those here tomorrow. . . . What? I don't care how much it costs, just get it here. Now, listen to me carefully, Frederick, if you want any more business from the Vanderlust family, then you'll come through for your sweet Victoria. Have I made myself perfectly clear? . . . Thank you, that's better. Now, about those French paintings, have them here by Friday and place the bronze statue that we selected in the garden room. I want this place looking perfect for my Polo Club luncheon in two weeks, and I'm depending on you to have everything right. *[doorbell rings]* And make sure the tea room is done in the latest colors. You know I have all new furnishings coming and . . . *[doorbell rings again; Victoria is a bit aggravated.]* Oh dear, I have someone at the door, and it looks like I'm going to have to answer it. Tah, tah, darling, and remember, if you keep Victoria happy . . . *[a soft laugh as she's listening]* Oh, you do understand. Good-bye. *[goes to door and opens it, there stands Marcia]* Oh, hello, it's you. . . . Let me see, you are . . . Martha . . . is that right?

MARCIA: Not exactly, Mrs. Vanderlust. My name is Marcia, and we've been living two doors down from you for about three years now.

VICTORIA:　*[oblivious to her insult]* Oh, yes, that place is such an eyesore in the neighborhood. Well . . . do come in.

MARCIA:　*[takes two steps, head down, trying to be very positive]* Oh . . . thank you very much.

VICTORIA:　*[cuts her short]* That's far enough. I'm in the midst of remodeling our little home. . . . After all, it's been six months since our last little face-lift around here, but I suppose you folks don't do that sort of thing, now do you?

MARCIA:　Well, we haven't had much to work with lately since my husband has been out of work, and it's been rather hard on me and the kids to make ends meet.

VICTORIA:　Yes, I suppose it is. Well, how can I help you today? And please make this request short, I'm one busy lady you know.

MARCIA:　Yes, Mrs. Vanderlust, I understand.

VICTORIA:　Oh, please call me Victoria. None of my friends are around to hear you, so please use my first name. It's from royalty you know.

MARCIA:　Well, I assumed that it probably was . . .

VICTORIA:　I assume you're here for the PTA, or the March of Dimes, or one of those fund-raisers . . .

MARCIA:　Well, not exactly—

VICTORIA:　*[cuts her off, takes control]* Now, now, I don't need to hear another word. My purse is right here. *[reaches for purse on table]* I'm always willing and ready to do my part for our little community. So, what can I do for the cause . . . *[She has pulled out several dollars that have fallen all over the floor.]* Oh, how clumsy of me to be so careless with all that money.

MARCIA:　*[Marcia reaches down to help and hands the dollars to Victoria]* Well, actually, it's not the PTA or the March of Dimes that brings me here today and . . . *[looks around]* maybe I've come to the wrong house. I think I've made a mistake, Mrs. . . . Victoria. Yes, I've made a big mistake. I'm sorry to have bothered you. If you'll excuse me, I'll be going—

VICTORIA:　What on earth are you chattering about? *[being analytical]* You came to my home, rang my doorbell, and here I am. You have something on your mind, so please, dear Martha, tell me what it is.

MARCIA:　It's Marcia.

VICTORIA:　Of course it is. . . . Now what can I do for you? If it's a job for your husband, I'm sure I can—

MARCIA: *[nervous and talks fast]* No, it's not a job for my husband. But I was wondering . . . only because our daughters are in the same class at school and because we do attend the same church . . .

VICTORIA: Oh really now?

MARCIA: . . . and, well, I was wondering, *[closes her eyes and speaks rapidly out of sheer terror]* could I borrow $2.00 for my daughter's school lunch? I didn't have anything to make her a lunch. I'll pay you back on Monday with tips from my part-time job at the diner and . . . oh, I'm so embarrassed. I just should have gone . . .

VICTORIA: Two dollars? What on earth for? Lunch was fifty cents . . . just a few years ago.

MARCIA: *[trying to excuse herself]* Thank you. I knew I shouldn't have come here.

VICTORIA: The lunch at the school costs $2.00? That's outrageous. Mr. Vanderlust and I are taxpaying citizens, and you can be sure we'll look into this matter. Two dollars is the most ridiculous thing I've ever heard. Why, no one has any respect for money these days. What are they feeding those children anyway?

MARCIA: Mrs. Vanderlust, I made a big mistake. I'll see myself out, thank you.

VICTORIA: Oh my, don't leave so quickly. After all, since we do go to the same church and our daughters are in the same grade, you said? Well, here's *[pulls out one dollar from her purse, protective of her purse]* a dollar. I'm sorry I don't have more, but things are a little tight this month with the remodeling and all. . . . I'm sure the Richies across the street can spare another dollar, or you may want to try that little church of ours. And I do hope you can solve your problems.

MARCIA: *[with a slight show of strength, gives the dollar back and speaks clearly]* That's okay, Mrs. Vanderlust. I can see you need this dollar more than I do. It clearly means an awful lot to you, and I can't take it from you. *[Victoria takes the dollar back and puts it into her purse.]* Good-bye . . . Victoria . . . and happy remodeling. Maybe we'll see you in church on Sunday. *[finds her way out alone]*

VICTORIA: *[offended]* Well, of all the ingratitude. You try to help someone out and they just can't receive a little kindness. *[indignant]* What is this world coming to?

[freeze; blackout]

4

Let Him Who Stole, Steal . . .

THEME

Stealing is more than shoplifting from a retail store or even taking the forbidden cookie from the cookie jar. Stealing goes much farther into the realm of reputation, trust, dreams, and more, as you will see in this drama sketch.

CHARACTERS

ALEX: Typical all-American male who is looking out for number one. He is dressed casually.

WENDY: Alex's girlfriend, who has been deeply wounded by Alex's inconsiderate and selfish actions. She is wearing sunglasses, coat, and scarf to not be recognized by others.

SETTING

A small café table and two chairs identifies this out-of-the-way scene for a couple to meet and have their discussion.

As music plays in the background, Wendy enters, carrying a cup of coffee and takes a seat at the table. She is nervous and obviously not comfortable with this meeting. Alex strolls on stage, knowing he's in trouble with Wendy. His I-don't-care attitude is more than obvious. The moment is very tense.

ALEX: *[carrying a cup of coffee, he responds to "people" in the café]* Hey, Ted, good to see you. Be sure to say hello to your parents; tell them I've missed them. *[finally breaks the ice after a moment of discomfort]* Hi, Wendy. *[no response, pause]* So . . . how was your day at work? *[She turns away.]* Do you want me to get you another cup of coffee? *[pause]* Look, you said we could talk, or are we going to have to read each other's minds?

WENDY: *[cold and very angry]* Look, Alex, I don't want another cup of coffee, and I certainly don't want anything from you. And as far as reading each other's minds, that's obviously your department, not mine. I had no idea how you were using me.

ALEX: *[defensive and sarcastic]* Oh, I get it. I was using *you! [forceful]* What happened to two consenting adults who both expressed, after six months of steady dating, that they were both "so much in love"?

WENDY: You talked me into it.

ALEX: I talked you into nothing. You were the one who was always talking about the future and marriage and kids and . . . and the all-American dream . . . which is turning into a nightmare.

WENDY: Alex Johnson, you've broken my heart.

ALEX: I broke your heart? And you think I don't have any feelings?

WENDY: And how am I supposed to know about *your* feelings when you never talk about them? Any feelings you have, you . . . you stole from me.

ALEX: *[sarcastic frustration]* Now, I'm a thief.

WENDY: You finally told the truth.

ALEX: Wendy, what have I stolen from you that you didn't give to me?

WENDY: *[painfully shared]* You stole my heart, Alex. . . .

ALEX: *[non-caring tone]* You offered.

WENDY: . . . you stole my thoughts and my dreams for the future.

ALEX: There was no future to steal.

WENDY: *[hard, slow, and deliberate]* And you stole my reputation.

ALEX: *[irritated, just as slow and deliberate]* I stole nothing.

WENDY: *[direct]* I heard what you told your "buddies" over at Tony's place last week.

ALEX: And how did you hear that?

WENDY: Does it matter? Alex, does anything matter with you? You get what you want and move along as if nothing happened. *[using his voice]* You always say, "This is no big deal," as long as no one gets hurt.

ALEX: *[easily enjoying the argument]* Now you're finally starting to make sense. You know that bit about no one gets hurt. . . . Well, I did nothing to hurt you.

WENDY: Alex, ever since I was a little girl I dreamed of a guy like you and all that a relationship could be . . . and I agree we made some bad choices. But you didn't have to tell the world.

ALEX: *[satirical]* Now my friends are the world.

WENDY: *[showing a lot of pain]* Alex, that really hurt. Now when I see *your* friends at the restaurant and *our* friends at work, they look at me as if I was some stupid idiot. Well, I guess I am stupid—stupid for ever trusting you. *Alex, you took things from me that I will never be able to get back.* I hope you're satisfied. Good-bye, Alex. *[Wendy starts to leave.]*

ALEX: *[trying hard, almost childish]* Hey, wait a minute, if you want your Walkman back just say so, and I promised you I'd replace your tennis racquet. What's the big deal?

WENDY: You just don't get it, do you, Alex? Like I said, to you nothing is a big deal . . . as long as you're getting what you want.

ALEX: So, I guess we . . . you and me are—

WENDY: *[finishes his sentence]* Finished, Alex. . . . D-O-N-E. . . . From me, Alex, you will steal no more. And the coffee is on me. *[Wendy throws some money down on the table and stomps off.]*

ALEX: *[Phone rings; Alex reaches into his pocket for his cell phone.]* This is Alex. . . . Hey, Sheila, what's happening? Busy? No, I'm not busy at all. In fact, I was hoping you'd call today. *[smooth act]* Sure, Sheila, I could . . . steal a little time out of my schedule. What the boss doesn't know won't hurt him. *[small laugh]* Look, I can meet you in twenty minutes, say at Tony's Café. . . . And listen . . . *[He picks up money on table left by Wendy.]* coffee is on me.

[freezes with a smile on his face; blackout; Music is played for the exit.]

5
He Is Not Coming

THEME

The second coming of Jesus Christ stirs many different emotions and expectations among believers and nonbelievers. Some believers are prepared for Jesus to come at any time. Another believer is skeptical. Among the unbelievers we find some interested and curious, while others have absolutely no belief in the coming of Jesus. This sketch shares some of those beliefs.

CHARACTERS

LYLE: The dad is a hard-nosed, in-your-face kind of guy. He is dressed in a sweater, dress slacks, and so forth.

LOUISE: The mom is kind and sweet, wearing her apron over a nice dress or slacks and sweater outfit.

JILL: A typical teenager dressed in updated fashion.

JACK: Jill's younger brother who is positive and curious. He is dressed in casual attire—khaki pants and a casual shirt that's nicer than a T-shirt.

SETTING

A dining room table decorated to the hilt for Thanksgiving with five chairs and five place settings. A couch is off to the side for the kids. A door stage right would be ideal.

Jill and Jack enter and sit on the couch to watch TV. Both Jack and Jill are bored to tears. Louise hums while she places plates on the table. Lyle enters to place a casserole dish on the table.

LYLE: *[places dish on center of table and begins to count the place settings nonverbally, then becomes very verbal with disgust]* three . . . four . . . and five. You just have to do this every year, don't you, Louise?

LOUISE: *[sincere]* Lyle, he's promised every year to come for Thanksgiving. And I'm going to be ready for him.

LYLE: *[building with a bent of anger]* And every year . . . for the past . . . thirteen years he's never shown his face once . . . not even once at this table. Why do you keep torturing yourself with . . . with an irresponsible old man who doesn't keep his promises?

LOUISE: *[still sincere]* Because he's my dad . . . and I love my dad . . . and I believe that just one of these days he's going to come through that door. *[hands him a fistful of silverware]* Here . . . just do the silverware, please. *[as she folds napkins]*

JACK: *[trying to be very fair and kind]* Jill, I think it's my turn to have the remote.

JILL: *[sarcastic and cutting]* Go away, bad dream.

JACK: *[arguing]* But you promised that on every odd number hour it would be my turn to use the remote control and choose the station I wanted.

JILL: *[forceful]* Well, the rules just changed.

JACK: *[angry]* But it's one o'clock.

JILL: *[teasing and mean]* The only thing odd here is you . . . and you're the odd man out because I have the remote.

JACK: *[whining]* Mom, Jill is changing the TV rules again.

LOUISE: Jill . . . remember what I said about how you act today. *[Jill throws the remote control unit at Jack.]*

JACK: So, do you think Grandpa is coming for dinner?

JILL: *[talks down to Jack]* No way. Didn't you hear Dad? Grandpa is never coming for dinner.

JACK: *[hopeful]* I'd really like to have Grandpa come . . . since I've never seen him.

JILL: You're not missing much.

JACK: *[positive]* I don't know. . . . He sends Christmas and birthday gifts every year, so he must be kinda cool.

JILL: *[sarcastic]* Grandparents are supposed to do that, dweeb. . . . Just watch your dumb program and staple your lips . . . okay? *[They both resume bored positions on the couch.]*

LYLE: You know, what your dad does every year . . . is just plain cruel. He makes all of these idle promises, builds up everyone's hopes, . . . gets you to do all of this extra work . . . for nothing . . . absolutely nothing.

LOUISE: *[apologetic]* Lyle, you know how busy Dad has been, and well . . . it just hasn't worked out for him to make it.

LYLE: Nothing works out with your dad. Think of our children. . . . Jill has seen him once . . . and Jack thinks he is some kind of Indiana Jones war hero who'll come waltzing in through the door with the ark of the covenant.

LOUISE: And if that's what Jack believes of my dad . . . then that's fine with me. Lyle, why do you have to make a big deal about this every year?

LYLE: Me? You're the one who sets a place setting for someone who's absent every year . . .

LOUISE: *[strong]* He may be absent to you . . . but he's not absent to me. *[pause]* Would you please call the kids to the table?

LYLE: Hey, you guys . . . it's time for dinner.

JACK: *[up right away and energetic, while Jill drags her way to the table]* So, is Grandpa coming, Mom?

LOUISE: I'm not sure, honey, but he might . . . and, well, *[energetic]* we're ready if he does.

JACK: Well, I sure would love to see him.

JILL: He's not coming, seed brain . . .

LYLE: Jill, that's enough. . . . But I'm afraid your sister is right, Jack, your grandfather is not coming for Thanksgiving.

LOUISE: *[to change the subject]* Lyle, would you please ask the blessing?

LYLE: *[offers hands to hold around the table and begins praying]* Dear God, thank You for our family and this food. And we give thanks for all that You have given us. In Thy name we pray. Amen.

JACK: *[immediately praying loudly]* And may Grandpa come to our house this Thanksgiving. Amen.

JILL: *[immediately]* He's never coming!

JACK: Is too.

JILL: Is not.

JACK: Is too, Mom said.

JILL: Is not, Dad said. *[Lyle is ready to speak, but Mom cuts in.]*

LOUISE: Children . . . *[to Lyle]* and you, too. . . . Can't we just have a peaceful dinner? . . . Now, somebody pass the rolls please. *[Doorbell rings; Jack looks at Mom while Jill and Dad look at each other.]* Well, Jack, . . . would you like to answer the door?

[freeze; blackout]

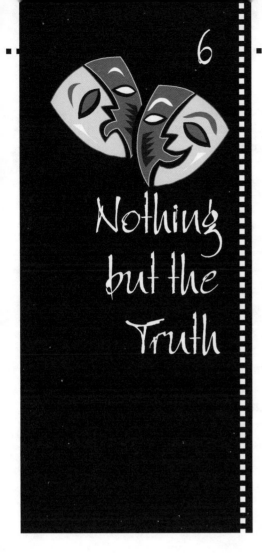

6

Nothing but the Truth

THEME

When we lie once, a second lie seems to follow, then more and more. The lie becomes a haunting voice that follows us everywhere. There is no escape except for one way—telling the truth, as we will see in this sketch with Brad and Jane.

CHARACTERS

BRAD: A liar, dressed in business attire.

JANE: Brad's loving and believing wife, dressed in very nice clothes.

LIE: Dressed in black from head to toe.

SETTING

A candlelit table and dinner served on fine china.

Jane is sitting at the table with dinner on, thumping her hand on the table and looking at her watch. It's obvious that Jane is not happy. Brad appears outside the door, disheveled and panicky. He is obviously late and guilty. He mimes his rehearsal of what he's going to say and then begins out loud.

BRAD: *[dramatic and trying to be sincere]* Ah . . . Jane, I had a flat tire on the expressway . . . and I'm so sorry I'm late. . . . No, I used that one last week. Let's see, ah . . . I had a late client that just would not leave the office. . . . *[looks up]* Oh, help me, somebody, help me. . . . *[new idea]* Ah, Dad called . . . and he's not doing well, and I just needed to listen to him. . . . Man, I'm busted—ten P.M. I'm dead. *[decisive and bold]* Nope, I'm going to tell the whole truth. . . . I just plain forgot about our anniversary dinner and my promise to be home on time. I was out with the guys. And would you forgive me? *[bolsters courage and comes in through the doorway]* Jane?

JANE: *[cool as a cucumber]* Hello, Brad!

BRAD: *[scrambling]* Sweetheart . . . love of my life. . . . I just have to tell you that I . . . the traffic was unbelievable and . . . and right in the middle of the expressway *[huge breath, pause]* I had a flat tire. Honey, it was awful—

JANE: *[not impressed]* Well, happy anniversary, . . . sweetheart, . . . and don't you honey me. *[gets up to leave]* Enjoy your cold steak and soggy vegetables and hard rolls that have been sitting here for four hours.

BRAD: But you just don't understand, I had a flat tire.

JANE: *[as she's leaving the room, unbelieving and a bit cynical]* A flat tire? . . . Just like last week and the week before . . . and the week before that. . . . *[counting on her fingers]* Let me see, four flat tires in four weeks. Brad, you need to quit your job and go work for Firestone. With all of your flat tires, the good Lord knows we can use the employee discount. And by the way, . . . *[grabs his hands and looks at them]* I'm amazed how you never get your hands dirty when you change a tire. Good night, Brad. And just once, it would be nice if you could tell the truth! *[She exits.]*

BRAD: *[trying to defend himself]* But . . . but . . . I . . . *[to himself]* I'm so . . . stupid. . . . I can't believe how I get myself in these messes. *[feeling a bit despondent]* I was just a . . . few hours late. . . . *[looks up to "heaven"]* Okay, four hours late. . . . Can't You give a guy a break. What have I done to deserve this? *[Brad places his head on the table. As he does, Lie appears and sits in the empty chair.]*

LIE: *[imitating Brad]* I had a flat tire.

BRAD: *[Brad looks up and straight ahead.]* What?

LIE: I had a flat tire.

BRAD: *[looks and sees Lie, jumps and reacts]* Hey, who are you and what are you doing in my house . . . at my kitchen table?

LIE: I had a flat tire.

BRAD: Look, pal, I have no idea who you are, but you better beat it or . . . *[makes a fist]* or face the consequences.

LIE: I had a flat tire. . . . Honey, it was awful.

BRAD: *[realizing what is happening]* Wait a minute . . .

LIE: *[like a broken record]* I had a flat tire.

BRAD: *[confident of who the Lie is]* You . . . you're my lie. Listen, . . . you better get out of here.

LIE: I had a flat tire.

BRAD: *[guilty and looking around to see if Jane is present]* Look, you're going to get me in trouble . . . now . . . just leave!

LIE: Honey, it was awful.

BRAD: *[loudly, gripping his ears]* Just stop it!!!

JANE: *[offstage]* Brad, who are you talking to?

BRAD: Ah . . . *[busted]* no one, sweetheart!

LIE: No one, sweetheart. *[laughs]*

BRAD: *[really nervous]* Look, I blew it. Now are you satisfied? Now will you go away?

LIE: I had a flat tire. Honey, it was awful. No one, sweetheart.

BRAD: *[sits down on the chair, grabs his ears to block out the noise]* What am I going to do? *[Lie sits next to him.]* It's obvious you're not going to leave me alone. *[puts head back down on kitchen table]*

JANE: *[walking back into the room, to bring him a cup of coffee]* Here, Brad. *[Offers cup and sees him in pain on the table]* Brad? Are you okay? I just wanted to say I'm sorry about getting mad at you.

BRAD: Jane . . . I need to tell you. . . . I didn't have a flat tire. . . . I . . . forgot about our anniversary . . . and I just faced my lie . . . big time. *[Lie gets up and steps back from the table and observes the conversation.]*

JANE: Brad . . . that's all I want to hear from you . . . the truth, the whole truth . . .

BRAD: Jane, you're wonderful.

JANE: Brad . . . remember where we had our first date? I think they're still serving those chili dogs. . . . What do you say we have dinner at that old diner down on seventh street.

BRAD: Let's go. . . . I love those chili dogs.

LIE: *[mocking]* I love those chili dogs.

BRAD: *[busted]* Ah . . . you know, I think I'll try the hamburger tonight.

[freeze; blackout]

7

Born Again? I Don't Think So

THEME

The idea of being "born again" provokes a lot of questions. What does it really mean to have a "new life," much less a new life in Christ? Is it an idea? A concept? Or a biblical imperative? This sketch takes a look at the second birth by making some comparisons with our first, natural birth.

CHARACTERS

JUNE ANDERSON: She is everywoman wearing casual clothes.

ALICE JEFFERSON: June's friend and is really pregnant.

SETTING

A park bench with a few ferns that create an outdoor setting.

June enters and takes a seat and begins to read a book. Alice struggles onstage to find the seat next to June.

ALICE: *[out of breath, holding her back]* Excuse me, but is this seat taken?

JUNE: *[never looking up]* Go ahead, its all yours. *[Alice slowly sits and groans on the way down, June sees who is sitting next to her, and speaks emphatically.]* Oh my, you are one pregnant lady.

ALICE: *[cynical]* Oh, and what was your first clue?

JUNE: Sorry, I just never saw anyone as big as you still walking around in public.

ALICE: *[surprised]* Well, it's nice to meet you . . . *[Look closely at each other and say each other's name at the same time.]*

ALICE/JUNE: June Anderson/Alice Jefferson.

ALICE: Class of _____ *[a graduating year: whatever is appropriate]*

JUNE: *[getting more excited]* Cheerleading squad.

ALICE: *[slowly gaining recognition]* "The Sound of Music."

JUNE:	Mr. Crabtree's math class.

JUNE/ALICE: Gary "The Lips" Waterman!

ALICE: So, what are you doing here?

JUNE: Just baby-sitting my nephew and catching up on some reading. *[looking at her stomach]* You look like you shouldn't be here.

ALICE: I know . . . two weeks overdue, and my doctor says I need to keep walking. *[groans with a pain]*

JUNE: Well, don't have it here, Alice . . . an ABJYN I am not.

ALICE: That's OBGYN and don't worry. *[awkward]* So, do you have . . . any . . . you know . . .

JUNE: *[finishes Alice's sentence]* Kids? Nope . . . tried for a few years . . . but gave up on that idea. The doctor said it would never happen. . . . *[cynical]* So Auntie June is the busiest baby-sitting aunt in _____. *[name a state]* And since my husband, Jerry, left me because he wanted to "sire a son," I have a lot of free time to baby-sit. *[pause, change of subject]* So, is this your first?

ALICE: *[jovial]* I wish . . . number three. *[squirms with a pain]*

JUNE: *[inquisitive]* Okay . . . tell me the truth. . . . Does it really hurt?

ALICE: Does what hurt?

JUNE: Having a baby. . . . Does it really hurt as bad as everyone says it does?

ALICE: *[laughs]* Take your *left leg,* put it over your right shoulder, then pull your *lower lip* up over your forehead . . . and tell me if that hurts.

JUNE: *[cringe of pain]* Oooo, so it really does hurt.

ALICE: *[contented]* But it's really worth it. My two kids bring me so much joy.

JUNE: *[forlorn]* I imagine they do.

ALICE: *[apologetic tone]* I'm sorry, June. I guess I wasn't thinking.

JUNE: No problem . . . *[changes subject and setting]* Um . . . does your family still go to that church you invited me to that one time?

ALICE: As a matter of fact, yes. My husband and I met there in our senior year of high school.

JUNE: It sounds like you still buy into all of that Christianity stuff.

ALICE: If what you mean is, have I been *born again*, the answer is *yes*.

JUNE: That wasn't quite what I was asking. *[beat]* But what do you mean by *born again?*

ALICE: Well . . . it's kind of like having a baby. And all you have to do is—

JUNE: *[cuts her off]* Wait a minute, if you want me to do that thing with my *left leg* and *lower lip* forget it.

ALICE: *[laughs]* No, that's not what I mean. But it does mean acknowledging God's Son, Jesus, as the one who went through a lot of pain . . . so that you and I could have a brand-new life.

JUNE: Let me get this straight . . . being *born again* . . . as you call it, doesn't require me to go through some strange hoops and crazy gymnastics to have a new life?

ALICE: You got it, June. Jesus did everything for you, so that you and I wouldn't have to go through that pain.

JUNE: Kind of like having a baby, huh?

ALICE: Trust me, I suffered through the childbirth a whole lot more than my kids suffered. They got life and I got two days in the hospital.

JUNE: It just sounds too simple.

ALICE: Well, it is simple, but it does mean *starting life all over again,* and for some people that's not very simple.

JUNE: Well, I sure could use a new life. This one hasn't worked out so well.

ALICE: It just requires simple faith in Jesus, in what He did for you.

JUNE: *[thinking]* I can't believe Jesus would do that . . . especially for me. I haven't been a very good person.

ALICE: June, do you know what Jesus said while He suffered to give you a new life?

JUNE: *[trying to be casual]* How about, *"Let's get this over with?"*

ALICE: *[laughs]* No, June, Jesus simply said, "It is finished." You don't have to do this yourself. June, Jesus really loves you.

[freeze; blackout]

8

Judge Not

THEME

Judging others is far too easy. No one had to teach us how to develop this human craft of holding erroneous views of others. God says, "Leave the judging to Me." We need reminders of that message from day to day.

CHARACTERS

FRANK: Our judgmental observer of the human condition. He is dressed rather casually, nothing matches, and he is wearing his binoculars. He can be politically incorrect.

CARL: The kind and nonjudgmental friend of Frank. He really wants to help Frank.

VOICE: Represents the voice of God's Spirit and comes through loud and clear.

SETTING

Open stage; no set items are needed.

As the music plays, Frank casually enters from backstage. He's using his binoculars to look at certain people in the audience as he makes his comments.

FRANK: *[stops on one person]* Wow, would you look at that? *[to another]* Oh my . . . oh my . . . oh my. *[to another]* Why . . . I would never have thought that. . . . *[to another]* Oooo . . . Blind my eyes from what I see. . . . *[to another]* Ah hah, I wondered about that . . . hmmmm. *[to another]* Golly, I had no idea! *[to Carl, who is sitting in the audience]* Whoa, that's my friend Carl, I thought he was a good guy. I sure never thought that he was messing around like that. . . .

CARL: *[Carl gets up and walks to the stage.]* Hey, Frank, what are you doing?

FRANK: *[still looking around at people in the audience]* Oh, hi, Carl!

CARL: What's with the binoculars?

FRANK: *[not wanting to give any information, but with a guilty tone]* Ah, what do you mean?

CARL: The spy glasses with all of your *ah ha*s and *ooo*s and *wow*s and stuff.

FRANK: *[still evasive]* Why do you ask?

CARL: Well, you got rather personal a moment ago.

FRANK: *[trying to get the upper hand]* Feeling guilty about something, huh?

CARL: Guilty . . . no—curious maybe. What *are* you doing?

FRANK: *[coy]* Just looking around.

CARL: Looking around at what?

FRANK: People.

CARL: Duh . . . that's obvious, Frank. So, what's with all of the comments?

FRANK: *[evasive]* What comments?

CARL: *[frustrated and direct]* Come on, Frank, you know what I'm talking about. . . . What are you seeing in those glasses?

FRANK: *[self-righteous and strong]* Garbage, Carl . . . I can see a lot of garbage.

CARL: *[totally confused]* Garbage? What are you talking about?

FRANK: *[hesitant]* Well, these are my super-duper sensational sin finders . . . by Mattel.

CARL: Sin finders? Frank, I think you've gone off the deep end.

FRANK: Someone has got to identify the sin in people's lives, and . . . well . . . I got the job.

CARL: Job? That's not your job.

FRANK: *[self-assured]* With these *[holds out binoculars]* I'm right.

CARL: *[very direct]* You are not right.

FRANK: *[bold]* I sure am. Here, *[hands binoculars to Carl]* take a look for yourself.

CARL: *[looks through binoculars]*

FRANK: *[smug]* So, what do you see?

CARL: *[factually]* People, with red, blue, and yellow sweaters; black and green jackets.

FRANK: *[stubborn, folding arms]* Not what I see.

CARL: *[with passion]* Then that means you're judging people and . . . in the wrong way.

FRANK: *[being coy]* Look, just because the glasses don't work for you—

VOICE: Stop judging by mere appearances. *[John 7:24]*

FRANK: Hey, did you hear that?

CARL: Hear what?

VOICE: Stop judging by mere appearances.

FRANK: *[excited and nervous]* There . . . he said it again.

CARL: *[confident]* Oh, that . . . sure I heard that.

FRANK: Well, who said that?

CARL: *[coy]* Who do you think?

FRANK: *[not willing to admit anything]* I . . . I'm not real sure.

CARL: Frank, you don't need binoculars—you need a hearing aid.

VOICE: Stop judging by mere appearances.

FRANK: There, I heard it again.

CARL: Frank, don't you remember when Pastor Joe read that verse from the Bible when we were kids?

FRANK: *[apologetic]* I guess I wasn't paying close attention.

CARL: *[gentle persuasion]* Maybe it would be a good idea to start listening, stop looking—and leave the judgment department up to God? *[Carl stands in a strong position with his hand out to receive the glasses.]*

FRANK: *[looking at him, speaks slowly with resignation]* I suppose you want me to give you—

CARL: The glasses, Frank. . . . Time to give up the glasses. *[He reluctantly hands the glasses to Carl.]*

FRANK: *[unhappy]* Now are you satisfied?

CARL: *[gesturing to the audience]* Now what do you see, Frank?

VOICE: Stop judging—

FRANK: I see nice people with *[takes a deep breath]* blue and green jackets.

CARL: And . . .

FRANK: *[forcing his new view a little]* And Jesus loves every one . . . of . . . us.

CARL: *[pleased]* I'm proud of you, Frank.

VOICE: Me too, Frank. *[shocked, looks up]*

[freeze; blackout]

9

Open Mouth, Insert Foot

THEME

Slander is the verbal effort to destroy another's reputation. It's done every day, and many have become experts. It is sad that many seem to enjoy the "sport" of slandering others. Slander, however, comes with a great price, as this sketch reveals.

CHARACTERS

MAXINE: She's not happy with her boss. Dressed in business attire, she is very forward, loud, and a bit brash.

ELIZABETH: The wife of Maxine's boss, but Maxine does not have a clue of the relationship. She is very kind and sweet, also dressed in business attire.

MR. GURNEY: Maxine's boss and Elizabeth's husband. He is dressed in a business suit.

SETTING

At stage center there is a simple table with four chairs representing a lunchroom in an office center.

Elizabeth is the first to appear onstage with a cup of coffee. Maxine follows closely behind.

MAXINE: *[formal, with an attitude]* Hello, my name is Maxine. . . . You must be new here.

ELIZABETH: *[timid]* Oh, hi . . . my name is Elizabeth. And, yes, this is my first time here. *[looking around]* You have a very nice lunchroom.

MAXINE: *[an edge to her comments]* It'll do. It's about time we got a nice one. It takes forever to get anything done around here.

ELIZABETH: *[surprised]* Oh, I didn't realize there was any difficulty in working here.

MAXINE: *[casual]* Hey, kid . . . don't worry about a thing. . . . I'll teach you the ropes. . . . Just follow me, and you'll skate through this place as if you were a gold medalist.

ELIZABETH: *[nervous]* Oh, well, thank you for the kind offer.

MAXINE: Hey, relax. . . . Just watch your *P*s and *Q*s and you'll be just fine. *[looks around to make sure no one is listening]* Just watch out for old man Gurney. Now there's a work of art.

ELIZABETH: *[trying to be clear]* Excuse me? Did you say Mr. Gurney?

MAXINE: No, I did not say MISTER Gurney. . . . I just said Gurney. You'll never hear me call him mister. A mister is the last thing that old coot is.

ELIZABETH: I didn't think he was *that* old.

MAXINE: Old??? Honey . . . that old man was the first one off the ark. And there wasn't another four-legged creature that would walk with him.

ELIZABETH: *[concerned]* Oooo, you don't like Mr. Gurney, do you?

MAXINE: You're new around here. So what was your first clue?

ELIZABETH: *[a bit shocked]* Well . . . I just thought that he was . . . well . . . I always thought that . . . maybe . . . you know, being the boss and all, I just assumed—

MAXINE: *[harsh and confident]* Assume the man is a jerk, sweetheart. Just keep your distance and stay out of his way. The man only thinks of himself. He's the most egotistical, self-consumed, control freak that ever walked on planet Earth.

ELIZABETH: I guess I don't know what I'm missing.

MAXINE: Missing . . . this guy is the missing link. His middle name has got to be Neanderthal.

ELIZABETH: *[bright-eyed and alert]* Well, I was just about to say that—

MAXINE: Say nothing . . . nothing needs to be said. I'll bet he reads books on how to intimidate and harass people. You know . . . he probably has a full-length mirror in his home to practice his scowls and his famous look that says, "You'll pay for this later." Keep your distance, kid, keep your distance.

ELIZABETH: *[kindly]* You know, I've met Mr. Gurney, and he didn't give me those impressions.

MAXINE: *[excited]* Impressions! The only impressions that guy knows how to give is an impression of Attila the Hun.

ELIZABETH: *[appearance of great concern and sympathy]* Oh, poor Mr. Gurney.

MAXINE: *[reflective]* Gurney. I'd love to see that man on a gurney . . . in the coroner's office.

ELIZABETH: *[playing along]* Oh, his poor family.

MAXINE: Now you're getting the picture. I'm just glad that I'm not married to the guy. . . . Can you imagine?

ELIZABETH: Well, actually . . . I was just about to tell you . . . *[Gurney walks up behind Maxine, unknown to her. He is carrying his coffee mug.]*

MAXINE: *[oblivious to her surroundings]* Why just last week, the guy enforces a new policy that everyone needs to bring their own coffee mug into the building so that the company doesn't have to buy any more Styrofoam cups . . . another one of his money-saving campaigns. *[As she turns in her chair, she sees Gurney, shrinks just a little, and begins to cover her last few lines, stumbling.]* And that's just what we want to do is save money, yes ma'am, every nickel we can. *[with full recognition]* Oh, MISTER Gurney, I was just sharing with Elizabeth how we're doing everything we can around here to save money.

GURNEY: *[playing along]* Well . . . thank you, Maxine, and good morning, Elizabeth.

MAXINE: Oh . . . you two know each other.

GURNEY: Yes . . . didn't Elizabeth tell you?

ELIZABETH: *[stands up to greet Gurney]* I've been trying to tell Maxine for the last five minutes, but she just had several other interesting comments about—

MAXINE: *[enthusiastically jumps in]* About our fine company and all of the benefits.

GURNEY: Yes, I'm sure. . . . Elizabeth, are you ready for lunch?

MAXINE: Oh, you two are having . . . lunch . . . together?

ELIZABETH: Yes, it's our first-month anniversary. . . . Would you care to join us, Maxine?

MAXINE: No thanks, I just had lunch—"roast employee-a-la-foot."

[freeze; blackout; music]

10

Hating You Is Hurting Me

THEME

Hatred is an awful malady that robs people of their joy and the fulfillment of life. In this sketch, Sharon hates her parents for very good reasons. It's unfortunate, though, that Sharon cannot get over the conviction that her parents really hated her and could not just love her.

CHARACTERS

SHARON: A young woman dressed nicely and casually. She needs to be able to adjust quickly from her past to the present. It would work well if she wore a ponytail at the beginning that she can quickly take out to look older in an instant.

FATHER: Dressed in a sweater and casual pants.

MOTHER: Can be in a skirt or slacks with an apron.

SETTING

A stool off to stage right.

Sharon is seated on the stool as Mother and Father are on either side in rather threatening positions. All are frozen until action begins.

FATHER: *[angry]* I can't believe this report card, young lady. What seems to be the problem?

SHARON: *[trying to defend herself]* I told you there's some mistake. That B should be an A-.

MOTHER: *[angry]* I told you to clean your room two weeks ago.

SHARON: *[trying to reason with her mother]* I haven't had time with all of the other stuff you have me doing.

MOTHER: What we have you doing? Seems to me you asked for piano lessons.

SHARON: Because you were embarrassed I didn't get a part in the first grade play.

FATHER: *[folds his arms and sulks]* And no thanks to the one who is paying for them.

MOTHER: And did we ask you to go to that expensive camp this summer?

SHARON: No, but you complained that you couldn't go to Europe because passage for three would cost too much.

FATHER: And again, no thanks for the *expensive* month at camp.

MOTHER: And that boyfriend of yours, when did you start dating that jerk?

SHARON: Right after you complained to your rich friends on the phone that your daughter would probably end up being an old maid.

FATHER: The boy's hair looks like a shag rug.

SHARON: I'm sorry he can't be like you.

MOTHER: *[mortified]* And do you have to work at that discount store?

FATHER: It's just not proper.

SHARON: *[defensive]* Look, you and your friends don't have to go there. Besides, they think I'm a very good employee, and I'll be on the cash register next week.

MOTHER: *[dreaming]* We had such high hopes for you.

FATHER: *[positively]* You could go anywhere and be anything.

SHARON: Have you ever considered that I don't need to go anywhere else, and I'm happy with who I am.

MOTHER: *[rapid fire, pressuring, and closing in on Sharon]* What you want is just not good enough.

FATHER: It's not the way we raised you.

MOTHER: *[moaning]* What will your grandparents think?

FATHER: *[angry]* What will we tell our friends?

MOTHER: Where will you live?

FATHER: Who will you marry?

MOTHER: How will you survive?

FATHER: Why do you keep torturing us like this?

MOTHER: You have no respect for *our* feelings.

FATHER: You have no respect for yourself.

SHARON: *[yells]* Just stop it! *[Parents both freeze.]*

SHARON: *[looks at her frozen parents and slowly walks to center stage]* That was about seven years ago. Do you see why I hate my parents? *[pulls out her ponytail]* I just don't want to be around them or have anything to do with them. Hatred for me simply means, you live your life and I'll live mine. You stay in your corner of the world and I'll stay in mine. *[reflective]* You know, it's sad that they'll never meet my husband, and they'll never know their granddaughter. They don't even know that I have my degree in social work and that I help poor people. *[little laugh]* The funny thing is that the people I help have stories just like mine. They couldn't measure up either. They were never loved and accepted by their parents. So they're filled with an ugly kind of hatred that never seems to go away. But I can't fix them, and trying to help them couldn't fix me. All of the fixing is already done. Too bad nobody can fix hate. Too bad I'll never see my parents again. They sure are missing out on a lot of good things. I just wanted them to love me for who I am.

[music; blackout]

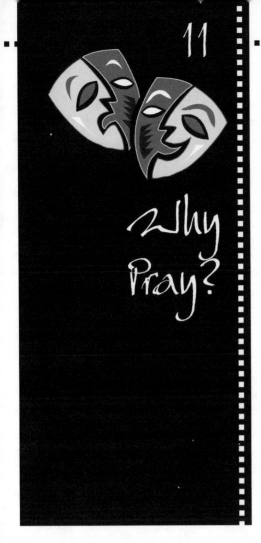

11

Why Pray?

THEME

Most everyone has questions about prayer. The greatest question is, "Is it even necessary to pray?" "Why bother?" some say. Many believe, since God is in charge, He will do what He pleases and really doesn't hear our personal requests.

CHARACTERS

MARY: Everywoman, who knows God, yet often forgets who God is and how He desires to work in our lives. She is in a bathrobe, hair net, curlers; later in slacks and sweater.

KATE: Mary's best friend, who knows God about as well as Mary and also doubts God's willingness to actually help her. She is open, however, to Mary's spiritual advice. She is in slacks and a sweater.

JODY: Everyone's waitress.

VOICE: Represents the voice of God.

SETTING

Scene 1:   Mary's living room at stage right is a simple easy chair with a side table and lamp.

Scene 2:   A small table and two chairs at stage left is a diner where Mary and Kate are served by Jody.

Director's Note: Scene 1 can stand alone without doing scene 2.

SCENE 1

Mary is sitting in her easy chair reading her book or magazine. One or two big and loud yawns interrupt her "concentration."

MARY: *[in bathrobe, making her last yawn]* Woooo, am I ever tired. I need to get to sleep. Five-thirty comes so early. *[swoons over book]* That Sydney Goodlove is such a good writer. But, it is nighty-night time. *[another yawn, puts book down, and is about to walk away, stretches and says]* Good night. *[as if to say it to the lamp or book]*

VOICE: *[kindly]* Good night.

MARY: *[hits the deck in fear, grabs an object or her book from the table as a potential weapon, then peeks out behind the chair and with courage yells . . .]* All right, mister. I have a weapon in my hand, and you'd better identify yourself real quick or I'll . . . I'll use it.

VOICE: *[hurt and with a kind tone]* You forgot who I am?

49

MARY: *[relaxes for a moment]* Rick, is that you? *[tightens up again]* Look, whoever you are, I'm dialing 911 right now. So you'd better leave.

VOICE: *[firm]* But, Mary, you're not holding a phone.

MARY: *[calling the bluff]* How do you know?

VOICE: *[parental]* Mary, I know you far too well.

MARY: *[irritated]* Bob, if that's you, this is *not* funny. We broke up a *long* time ago.

VOICE: Mary, this is not Bob or Rick!

MARY: *[in awe]* Then . . . that . . . leaves only . . . *[She looks up, rather disappointed.]* You!

VOICE: *[cheerful]* Good girl, Mary, I knew you'd remember Me.

MARY: *[a look of disgust]* Yea, well, why should I?

VOICE: *[sincerely]* Well, because . . . I love you.

MARY: *[cynical]* Yeah, well, You sure have a funny way of showing it.

VOICE: I'm sorry you're disappointed, but you know, I've missed our talks each night.

MARY: Well, what good are they? You never responded . . . until . . . now.

VOICE: But I did respond, just . . . not the way you wanted Me to.

MARY: Okay, was asking You for a nice evening with Elroy such a big deal?

VOICE: Elroy was not My will for you, Mary. He would have only hurt you. And you know how Elroy feels about Me!

MARY: *[ticked]* Well, giving me the hives on our first date was a funny way of telling me not to date Elroy. . . . Okay, okay, You win. . . .

VOICE: I didn't know this was a contest.

MARY: *[overly confident on this one]* All right, what about those two weeks I was in the hospital with Z E R O in the checkbook. *[pushing a little]* Huh? Huh? What was your response then? I only asked that You supply our needs and see me and the kids through those tough days.

VOICE: You're right, Mary, I didn't give you any cash. *[Mary responds, self-assured.]* But don't you remember the people I sent you with the meals, and the neighbor who paid your utility bills, and the men from church who fixed your car, and the doctor—

MARY: *[short]* All right, you came through. *[Pause, Mary begins to think hard about other ways that God has let her down.]* Okay, I got one more.

VOICE: Fire away.

MARY: *[overly confident]* I've got You this time. Remember that flat tire on Highway 12 on my only vacation last year?

VOICE: I remember it well.

MARY: And well You should. You knew I didn't have a spare tire in my trunk. And I just got done asking You to give me a nice vacation.

VOICE: And I tried to get the word to you that the flat tire actually protected you from a horrible accident around the next corner. But you were so angry at Me that you just went back home, and well, we haven't talked since.

MARY: *[almost apologetic]* That flat tire was for my good?

VOICE: The nail in the road was Mine . . . and I also arranged the tow truck to help you out of the ditch. *[Mary groans with head in her hands.]* It wasn't good luck like you thought.

MARY: *[Mary looks up, humbled.]* God, could we start over?

VOICE: I'd sure like that. *[Mary bows to pray.]*

[Music plays softly as lights dim to go out.]

SCENE 2

Mary and Kate enter and sit at a small café table.

KATE: *[upset]* Mary, I just don't know what I'm going to do. My boss was so cruel in how he fired me.

MARY: *[bewildered]* I'm so sorry, Kate. Why those . . . *[Jody walks up.]* Men! Oooooo those . . . men!

JODY: *[matter-of-factly]* Sorry, ladies, men are not on the menu, but we do have a special on the turkey sandwich.

MARY: I'll have the taco salad.

KATE: I'll have the chili enchilada.

JODY: One taco salad and chili enchilada. *[She exits.]*

KATE: Mary, you've been through so much and turned out so . . . strong and everything seems to come together for you. What should I do? *[Kate freezes.]*

VOICE: Mary, tell her to pray for My will, remember?

MARY: *[Mary responds awkwardly.]* What, and tell her she's going to probably end up getting hives . . .

KATE: *[confused]* Mary? Excuse me, what did you say?

MARY: Ah . . . Lives . . . we need to ask God to help us with our lives.

KATE: Oh, Mary, I wish I had the faith you do . . . but prayer never seems to accomplish anything. *[Jody comes up with food.]* It's like talking to this fork.

JODY: So we're talking to the fork, are we? Are you sure you don't want the turkey special? *[Jody and Kate freeze.]*

VOICE: Mary, remind Kate I will supply all her needs, just like I did for you.

MARY: *[to God]* But that was different, I was in the hospital.

JODY: Okay . . . and maybe you need to return to the hospital. . . . Look, ladies, anything you need? . . . Don't ask, *[leaving]* please don't ask.

KATE: Mary . . . are you okay?

MARY: I'm fine, Kate . . . but I have to say, God will meet all of your needs, even without a job. . . . I can't tell you how He's going to do it, but I promise, Kate . . . He will.

KATE: But, Mary, I'm so afraid. . . . I don't know what to expect around the corner. I've never been down this road before.

MARY: I think I have, Kate. *[chuckles]* I think I have, and I ended up with a flat tire.

KATE: I don't understand, Mary.

MARY: That's okay . . . trust me. . . . And I'm going to pray for you, even if you can't pray yourself . . . and even though it doesn't seem like it will ever happen, God will come through, Kate. *[reaches out for Kate's hand]* He always does.

[freeze; blackout; music out]

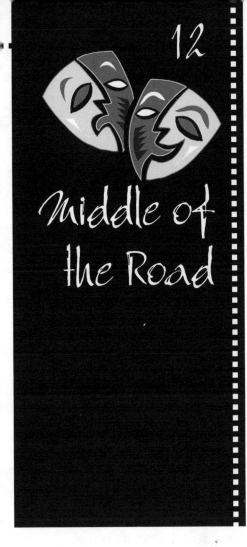

middle of the Road

THEME

If honest, most believers would admit to living their faith in the "middle of the road." That's where many feel comfortable and even justify that position. That's dismaying to those who would love to have someone stand strong for what they believe.

CHARACTERS

RICH: Our "cold" Christian. He is a skilled craftsman, dressed in work clothes.

DAVE: A nonbeliever. He is open and honest about his nonbelief, and he's here to party-hearty. He is dressed much like Rich. He ultimately wishes Rich would stand up for his faith.

JOE: A secret believer. No one knows that he's a Christian. He's totally silent about his faith, and it is a surprise at the end that Joe is a Christian. He is dressed as the others.

SETTING

Casual lunch table at work with several chairs.

As music plays, Dave and Joe enter, sit, and freeze as they begin to open their bag lunches or lunch pails. Rich enters to talk to the audience as he gives information about his two friends.

RICH: Hi, folks, my name is Rich—Rich Anderson. Welcome to the lunchroom at ABC Electronics. This is where I work, and these are my two best friends, Dave and Joe. *[walks behind Joe and Dave as they remain frozen]* I'd like to introduce them to you and explain a few things before we begin our lunch hour. First of all, you need to know that I'm a Christian and attend a really great church. *[puts his hand on Dave's shoulder]* Dave here is a not a Christian and doesn't intend to be, and you'll figure that out as you hear him speak in just a moment. *[walks over by Joe]* Joe? I'm not sure where Joe is at in his relationship with God, so I kind of tread lightly. You see, I have to be careful about sharing my faith at work. I can't be too pushy. You know what I mean. *[sits with the other two and begins to open his lunch]* So I'm sure you'll understand how I have to respond to my friends. *[then bows for a prayer]*

DAVE: *[mocking]* Hey, Rich, got something in your eye?

RICH: Yah . . . yah . . . allergy season. Itchy eyes, runny nose . . . you know.

JOE: *[making small talk]* Lot of that going around, why my wife—

DAVE: *[jumps in real excited]* Hey, guys, did you see that new babe working in the shipping department?

JOE: Wow, what a knockout! *[giddy]* What do you think, Rich?

[Dave and Joe freeze.]

RICH: *[to the audience]* Now, folks, I have a choice to be human or be spiritual. Remember, I can't be too pushy and rub these guys the wrong way. Remember, I have to protect my testimony. *[to Dave and Joe who come alive]* Do you mean the young lady with the red hair?

DAVE: *[mocking]* What a ditz. You need glasses man. Why she's as blonde as that Baywatch babe. *[Dave and Joe freeze.]*

RICH: *[to audience]* You see, I just use the old avoidance tactic. Works like a charm. *[to Dave and Joe]* Sorry, guys, I guess I am not plugged in like you guys.

JOE: *[curious and leading]* Hey, Dave, I hear Larry Maxwell just got engaged. And I heard there's going to be a little bachelor party.

DAVE: *[enthused]* The party of the century is next Saturday at my place. The booze is going to flow like a river, and the videos will be handpicked by Dave. Now, I can count on you guys being there, right?

JOE: *[affirming]* Wouldn't miss it for anything, man. Hey, you can count on me.

RICH: *[huge hesitation]* Wow, I'd love to come, but me and the Mrs. are already committed for next Saturday night.

DAVE: What? Don't tell me that you have to go to one of those church deals?

RICH: No, just a family reunion. Sorry, can't break the family commitment. *[Dave and Joe freeze; Rich addresses the audience.]* Now, you know as well as I that I don't have a family reunion. But as you can see they know I go to church, and I can't be caught dead at . . . their party. So, a little white lie keeps me in good graces and protects my testimony. *[to Dave and Joe]* So what do you guys think about those _____? *[name a professional sports team]*

DAVE: *[ignores the question]* Come on, Rich. Just tell your wife that you can't make the reunion thing and for once your buddies come first. Your family will make it without you, and your church will forgive you the next time you plant one of those big checks in the plate. Right, Joe?

JOE: You got it, Dave. Come on, Rich, time to hang with the guys.

[Dave and Joe freeze.]

RICH: *[to the audience, a bit more defensive this time]* Okay, now what would you do? *[begins to leave his seat and walk down stage center]* And don't tell me you haven't been in this jam before. There's a lot of pressure trying to be a Christian and get along in this dog-eat-dog world. You've got to play both sides of the fence. *[Rich freezes and Dave comes alive.]*

DAVE: *[comes up to Rich and speaks to the audience with a tone of sarcasm]* Look at him. He's become a pro at playing both sides of the fence. And don't think I haven't heard a word he's said. I'm not dumb, and he isn't the first so-called Christian that's worked here. Actually, I love to push this guy. It's kind of fun to watch him squirm and make up stuff to protect this thing called his "testimony." You know, I really wish he could be honest and stand up for his faith in God. That would be impressive. That is, if he really has faith in God. *[Dave freezes.]*

JOE: *[comes out rather shyly]* Well, I think I have them both fooled. Dave thinks I'm just like him. Rich thinks I need to get right with God. And you . . . you think I'm just the guy who follows along. Well, to be honest, I'm a Christian, too. Gave my life to Christ several years ago. But I haven't told anyone . . . until now. So, what do I do? I guess I have a choice to be like Dave or Rich. Frankly, neither choice is very appealing. But for now, I guess I'll keep my mouth shut. Besides I'm not hurting anyone. *[freeze]*

[Lights go out; music plays all three offstage.]

13

Who's Afraid?

THEME

Everyone struggles with some level of fear. Some struggle more than others, as seen in this sketch. Overcoming fear is not an easy task. Yet, there is help, but only when there is love, for *"Perfect love casts out all fear."*

CHARACTERS

JOE: Represents everyman, full of life and energy. Dress is casual. Joe and Cindy are an engaged couple.

CINDY: Represents a very paranoid, overreactive, and emotional person. She is dressed casually.

SETTING

Stage left needs two chairs, an end table, and a phone. Stage right needs an end table and phone. A door can separate the two.

As music plays, Cindy enters and cautiously approaches a chair at stage left while Joe, seated at stage right, confidently picks up and dials the phone.

CINDY: *[Phone rings and Cindy jumps, nervously speaks before answering.]* I wonder who that could be? *[panics]* It's only a little after six P.M. and no one calls me after six. It could be my mother or father, and something bad has happened. *[showing enormous fears]* It's probably a car accident or worse. Maybe my house is burning and the neighbor is trying to call me and warn me to get out. *[beset with fear]* I don't know what to do. *[closes her eyes with hand on phone]* Okay, I'll answer it . . . but only this time. *[picks up receiver, speaks timidly]* Hello?

JOE: *[upbeat]* Hey, Cindy, this is Joe.

CINDY: *[nervous and unusually cautious]* Joe who?

JOE: *[confused]* Cindy? This is Joe, your fiancé. Remember, the guy who proposed to you three years ago and you are planning to be married next month?

CINDY: How was I to know that? You just said Joe. There are millions of Joes in the world! You could have been a serial mass murderer calling from your cell phone in front of my house just to see if I was home.

JOE: Cindy, can I come over?

CINDY: But, Joe, it's after six o'clock. Why do you need to come over now?

JOE: I have plans for our honeymoon trip, and I want to share them with you.

CINDY: Well . . . okay. . . . But please be careful. . . . There are cars on the road and be careful of children playing alongside of the street.

JOE: *[kind and confident]* I'll see you in about fifteen minutes. Bye. *[Joe hangs up the phone, gets up from his seat, and walks toward Cindy's set, and freezes while she continues on the phone.]*

CINDY: *[nervous]* Be careful and watch your speed. If you speed, your insurance will go up, and if you lose your insurance and get in an accident then you'll lose your home, and if it hits the newspapers you'll lose your job, and then we won't be able to get married, and I'll end up all alone for the rest of my life. *[pause]* Hello? Are you there? Oh no . . . he's not answering. I hope he didn't faint or stop breathing. *[A knock at the door, Cindy jumps, frantic.]* I knew something would happen to Joe. I bet it's the police right now telling me that Joe has had a seizure, or . . . or he's had a serious accident and he's in the hospital. . . . Oh why do these things always happen to me? *[gets up to answer the door, closes eyes or places one hand over her eyes, and opens the door and speaks in her melodramatic tone]* Go ahead, tell me what happened to Joe.

JOE: *[trying to be dramatic]* Well, madame, Joe drove his car over a cliff and fell into the ocean and sharks devoured anything that was left.

CINDY: *[melodramatic]* I knew it. . . . I was afraid Joe would be . . . de . . . voured by . . . sharks. . . . *[opens eyes]* Oh, you!

JOE: *[trying to be positive]* Hey, relax, I'm here, and I didn't get a speeding ticket.

CINDY: *[unemotional]* Come on in and tell me about our honeymoon trip.

JOE: *[excited]* This is going to be the trip of a lifetime. *[pulling out brochures to show Cindy]* First we fly to Detroit and then to Miami.

CINDY: What? You know I'm afraid of flying.

JOE: Cindy, it's just one time . . . these are big planes.

CINDY: That means they fall faster and harder.

JOE: *[trying to ignore her]* Then we board the Norwegian Cruise ship and go to our first island near Nassau.

CINDY: Cruise ship? Didn't you watch Gilligan's Island. There's no way you're getting me on a three-hour tour. And the Bermuda triangle is out there. Are you trying to get rid of me?

JOE: Cindy, there's nothing to fear. Look, we'll be staying in the Hilton right on the beach.

CINDY: On the beach? Haven't you heard of tidal waves? We'll be the victims of a hurricane, and there goes the honeymoon.

JOE: *[firm]* Cindy, it's not going to happen. What are you so afraid of?

CINDY: *[strong]* Afraid of? Look, Mr. No-Fear, why should we be exempt from every catastrophe?

JOE: *[concerned]* And why should we experience *every* catastrophe?

CINDY: *[sulking]* I can't help it; I'm afraid.

JOE: Look, doesn't the Bible say, "Perfect love casts out all fear"? Well, I love you, so you don't have to be afraid.

CINDY: *[firm]* Thanks, Joe, but I'm not flying.

JOE: *[trying very hard]* How about driving to Miami?

CINDY: *[She goes crazy again.]* Drive? Do you realize how many fatal car crashes happen on American highways each year . . . each day?

JOE: *[calling her bluff]* Cindy . . .

CINDY: *[resigned]* Okay . . . I'll fly because . . . you love me. But we go to Disney and no roller coasters.

JOE: *[smiles and laughs]* Fair enough. You've got a date . . . and a honeymoon.

[freeze; blackout]

14

Totally Dependent

THEME

We really don't know what it is to be totally dependent upon God. Too often, we place our dependency in our resources, others, or ourselves. God is usually the last one we depend upon.

CHARACTERS

OG: Our early-first-century man, dressed in a simple tunic.

GROG: Og's friend, dressed similarly.

CLOG: Grog's friend, dressed similarly. Clog represents the believer in God.

SETTING

A simple set with rocks, or simple bench, or some place to sit is all that is needed.

Director's Note: If the names in this sketch become too difficult for the actors to perform, change them to other names, such as Fred, Barney, and Bob.

As the music plays or a simple drum cadence matches the footsteps, Og enters to stage center and, after a big breath, finds a seat. Grog and Clog enter shortly after and the three greet each other. Each begins very positively and supportive of one another.

OG: *[energetic]* Greetings, my friend, Grog.

GROG: *[pleasant]* Good day, Og, and here comes our friend Clog.

CLOG: *[carrying a scroll under his arm, chipper]* Hello, Grog and Og.

GROG: Clog, what a beautiful day today.

OG: *[inquisitive]* Clog, what is that you're carrying?

CLOG: Oh, a new edict from King Bog.

OG: *[critical]* I wish King Bog would mind his own business.

GROG: *[negative]* I agree, he's always sitting around thinking of some new rules or ideas for us to obey.

OG: Well, I'm tired of obeying.

GROG: And I'm tired of paying . . . all those taxes.

CLOG: *[positive]* Not me, I do everything the king asks me to do.

OG: *[derogatory]* Meaning you don't have a mind of your own.

GROG: *[chiming in with Og]* Nor do you have the sense to make your own way in this world.

CLOG: Well, I just thought as citizens of TOG we should listen to King Bog.

OG: *[with a touch of great insight]* Listen to us banter. Are we not capable of being kings ourselves?

GROG: *[agreeing]* Of course we are. We can think like a king, reason like a king, and act like a king. *[Mimes a royal position]*

OG: Indeed, why should it be King Bog when it could be King Og.

GROG: *[making a point]* Or King Grog.

OG: *[proudly making a point]* Far better King Og than King Grog.

GROG: *[argumentative]* I disagree, Og; you are not king material . . . like I am.

OG: I beg to differ.

CLOG: Whoa, guys, Og, Grog, take it easy. That's why we have one king, King Bog. As you can see there's no room in this kingdom for more than one king.

OG: Then we'll have separate kingdoms.

GROG: *[commence arguing]* Indeed, I will establish mine to the east and you go west.

OG: *[raising his voice]* I will not go west, for I favor the east.

GROG: *[loud]* You will go west.

OG: *[nose to nose, louder]* I will not.

CLOG: *[interrupting, steps between with a yell]* Guys, stop this. You'll destroy each other if you keep this up.

Og: Then let the destruction begin.

Clog: *[calmly]* I think it already has. Can't we just learn to trust King Bog? Besides, I thought you guys were friends.

Og: *[turns his back to Grog]* Not if he has to be king.

Grog: *[also turning away]* There will be no friendship if he is king.

Clog: *[showing strength between them]* Then you will both live lonely and very miserable lives. As for me, I will stay in the kingdom of Tog and obey King Bog, *[unwraps scroll]* who by the way says *[reads scroll]*

> To all my royal subjects.
>
> A great feast will be held for all the people.
>
> My son, the royal prince has been born.
>
> Come and celebrate this day at the palace.

Well, see ya guys, I am going for the free food and fun. Enjoy your new kingdoms.

Og: *[with his back still toward Grog, now trying to break the ice]* Grog, are you still there?

Grog: *[trying to be tough, but not doing well]* Of course I'm here.

Og: So, what are you going to do?

Grog: I'm not sure.

Og: Me neither. I must think and reason for myself. *[freeze]*

Grog: And that's what I must do as well. *[freeze]*

Clog: *[enters again stage center]* The rest of the story goes like this: Og and Grog spent the rest of their lives trying to be kings, but they never succeeded, never enjoyed life in the kingdom, and basically made a fine mess of everything. As for me, it was a great feast; and King Bog, he is wonderful.

[Music plays and Clog walks off, followed by Og and Grog.]

15

Hope for Tomorrow

THEME

When we go through tough times, we desperately need hope. That is the case of Cindy and her mom. They have lost everything and have lost all hope. All that remains are the prayers of a distant grandmother.

CHARACTERS

MOM: In her middle thirties or early forties and dressed very poorly with less than the best of hairstyles or makeup.

CINDY: About seven to ten years old, dressed poorly with nothing that matches. She is carrying a shabby-looking doll.

SETTING

At center stage appear a short row of simple folding chairs.

Mom and Cindy enter, holding hands. Mom is carrying a clipboard and Cindy is carrying her doll. They slowly and timidly find their way to two of the chairs onstage.

MOM: *[kindly]* Cindy, just sit here while I fill out these forms.

CINDY: *[looking around with some disgust]* I don't think I like this welfare place.

MOM: *[conciliatory voice]* Well, for right now, it's going to have to be okay.

CINDY: *[inquisitive]* Mom, are you going to have those forms done before it gets dark outside?

MOM: Well, I should. Why do you ask?

CINDY: I just don't want to go back to that shelter place in the dark. That place kind of scares me.

MOM: *[regret-filled]* I'm sorry, honey, but we should be able to get back before dark.

CINDY: Mom?

MOM: What, honey?

CINDY: *[angry]* I don't like *[stumbles with the word]* foreclosure.

MOM: *[in agreement]* And I don't like it either.

CINDY: *[playing with her doll]* It takes away your best dolls and nice clothes and swing set and best friends.

MOM: *[reflective]* And our dreams, and hopes, and all of our—

CINDY: *[cuts her off]* Mom, when am I going to get some new clothes?

MOM: *[uncertainly]* Ah . . . tomorrow, honey, tomorrow. That's why I need to fill out these forms.

CINDY: You said "tomorrow" yesterday, Mom. *[pause]* You know what else I don't like?

MOM: *[into her form]* What else, Cindy?

CINDY: *[upset, while she plays with doll's hair]* I don't like divorce. *[Mom just looks at Cindy with a sigh.]* I miss Daddy. Do you miss Daddy?

MOM: *[firm, but kind]* Now, what did we promise each other this morning?

CINDY: *[trying hard to sell an idea]* That we were going to have ice cream today?

MOM: *[consoling]* Well, I did say that, but think again.

CINDY: *[resigns to fact]* That we were not going to talk about Daddy today. *[pause, now angry]* Mom, I don't like Tommy Feiger!

MOM: *[surprised]* Why do you say that?

CINDY: *[wounded]* Cause he called me a name that I can't tell you, and he said it's because we're poor.

MOM: *[defensive]* You just tell Tommy that we are not poor, and we're going to be back on our feet . . . real soon.

CINDY: *[hopeful]* Like tomorrow, Mom?

MOM: *[confident tone]* Yes . . . yes . . . like tomorrow!

CINDY: Mom?

MOM: *[firm]* Cindy, if you keep asking me questions we'll never get out of here before dark.

CINDY: I know, but what did Grandma mean when she said she would pray for us? Didn't she say that before?

MOM: *[reminiscent]* Yes, she did. She said she would pray after the *accident* . . . and after the *surgery* . . . and she said she would pray after the *divorce* . . . and after the *foreclosure.*

CINDY: Do Grandma's prayers work?

MOM: Actually, God has been good to us . . . during all we've been through.

CINDY: Mom? Are we going to get ice cream today?

MOM: Maybe tomorrow, honey, maybe tomorrow.

CINDY: *[upset]* Mom? I don't think I like tomorrows.

MOM: *[curious]* Why do you say that?

CINDY: *[with certainty]* 'Cause they never come. *[Cindy plays with her doll, then leans over and prays.]*

MOM: *[looks over at Cindy]* Cindy, what are you doing?

CINDY: Asking God for ice cream.

[Freeze; blackout; music plays them offstage.]

A Modern God

16

THEME

God has made man in His image. God, however, is often made in man's image(s). This sketch reminds us how we try hard to make God look and act the way we want Him to. Or we think God is just an image of our religious history and personal experience. Our images obviously fall far short.

CHARACTERS

TIM: He is casually seated at a desk, trying hard to fashion an image out of wood, stone, or clay.

AL: Tim's friend who tries to share that there is a God who is not seen. (It becomes obvious that they both have the wrong idea.)

SETTING

A stool with a small stand and an object to "make god."

As the music plays, Tim enters and works on his image. He may hum or ad-lib a few lines while Al comes by to begin the dialogue.

AL: *[chipper and friendly]* Tim, my man, how ya doin'?

TIM: *[intent in his work]* Oh . . . hi, Al, doing fine, thanks.

AL: *[looking curiously]* Hey, ah . . . what are you working on, pal?

TIM: *[casually]* Oh, just making . . . a god.

AL: *[laughs]* You know, I thought I heard you just say you're "making a god." *[nervous laugh]*

TIM: *[clear]* You heard correct, Al.

AL: *[a bit of shock]* Wait a minute, let me see if I have this straight? You're working with a piece of _____ *[material]* and you're calling that . . . god?

TIM: *[confident tone]* Seeing is believing. *[holds object up or points proudly to it]* What do you think?

69

AL: *[looks with disbelief]* God?

TIM: *[confident and proud]* god!

AL: *[trying hard to figure this out, feeling awkward]* God.

TIM: *[same level of confidence]* god!

AL: *[struggling]* But, can you talk to your god and does he answer?

TIM: You mean prayer?

AL: Yeah, I mean prayer.

TIM: I tried that before, and you know that doesn't work. So to answer your question, yes, you can talk to my god, and he doesn't have to answer unless you want him to.

AL: *[struggling more]* But . . . your god just sits there. He can't do anything.

TIM: *[an edge in his tone]* So what's your point?

AL: Why have a god if he doesn't do anything?

TIM: And I suppose your God is doing something? Come on, Al. That God who's down at that church you attend? When's the last time he did anything for you?

AL: *[scrambling]* Well . . . there's that one time when He . . . *[thinking]* I . . . I . . . I know when Betty was in the hospital God . . . *[trying hard to persuade]* Okay, that one time when Jimmy fell off his bike . . . *[drifts off sentence]*

TIM: See, Al, your God is no better than mine. You pray, sing, and read from His Book, but don't get any more results than I do. So what's the difference?

AL: *[upset]* Well, there's a big difference. *[tries hard to think]*

TIM: *[long awkward silence while Al is thinking and Tim is working . . . Tim finally breaks the silence very casually.]* So what's the difference? I'd really love to hear.

AL: *[trying harder than ever to make his faith work]* Well, my God is personal.

TIM: *[holds up the image]* So is mine.

AL: And my God is real.

TIM: *[taps on it to make a noise]* So is mine.

AL: *[almost beside himself, then pulls himself together and makes a wonderful speech]* Tim, God loves me . . . and you, and came to earth take away all my sins, and rose to give me hope of eternal life.

TIM: *[a bit of silence, then Tim sits back and looks seriously at Al]* You know, Al, we've been friends for a long time.

AL: About fifteen years.

TIM: *[curious and very deliberate]* Then, how come you never told me that before?

[freeze; blackout]

THEME

When bad things happen to good people, how does God respond? Is He angry? Is He upset? Or does He simply grieve (Eph. 4:30), or groan and hurt (Rom. 8:26)? This sketch reveals a God who really cares and hurts for those who go through tough times.

CHARACTERS

MICHAEL: An angelic being dressed in white.

GABRIEL: An angelic being dressed in white.

VOICE: Represents the voice of God offstage.

SETTING

At stage center there is a bench or a couple of chairs with a TV on a stand in front of them. The place is heaven.

As the lights come up, our two angels are looking at a TV monitor, eating popcorn, and drinking sodas as if they are watching a sporting event, but they are actually viewing the horrible events on planet Earth. They comment with amazement that these things could be happening.

GABRIEL: *[excited and upset]* Can you believe what just happened? Look at that.

MICHAEL: *[agreement]* That's the worse thing that I've ever seen.

GABRIEL: You know, just when you think things are going well . . .

MICHAEL: *[jumps in]* . . . the worse thing happens.

GABRIEL: *[pause, saddened]* You know, he was one of my favorites.

MICHAEL: Mine, too, everything was going so well for him. . . .

GABRIEL: . . . and his family.

MICHAEL: *[inquisitive]* Do you think that he did something to deserve this kind of treatment?

GABRIEL: No way. We've been watching him like hawks. He was nearly perfect.

MICHAEL: *[shaking their heads with sadness]* He had the best training.

GABRIEL: Came from a great home.

MICHAEL: Top of his class.

GABRIEL: All-pro.

MICHAEL: He was on the top-ten list . . .

GABRIEL: . . . along with the most likely to succeed.

MICHAEL/
GABRIEL: Go figure.

MICHAEL: Now he's lost everything.

GABRIEL: His business is a disaster.

MICHAEL: He's in financial ruin.

GABRIEL: He lost his home . . .

MICHAEL: . . . not to mention his standing in the community.

GABRIEL: *[full of remorse]* His children were killed so tragically.

MICHAEL: And look . . . look how his friends are treating him. I mean it really looks like he messed up.

GABRIEL: But we know he didn't.

MICHAEL: Gabriel?

GABRIEL: Yeah, Michael?

MICHAEL: Why do you think God allowed all of this to happen to His servant Job? I mean he is the best.

GABRIEL: I can only imagine to teach the rest of those humans some pretty tough lessons.

MICHAEL: *[pause, inquisitive]* Gabe? How do you think God feels about all of this?

GABRIEL: *[wondering]* I'm not sure.

MICHAEL: *[inquisitive]* Do you think He's angry?

GABRIEL: *[sincere]* No, Michael, I think He's heartbroken.

MICHAEL: *[agreeing]* I think you're right.

GABRIEL: I know He's grieving about all of this.

MICHAEL: *[amazed]* It's really tough to see God cry over these human beings.

GABRIEL: Tell me about it, especially after they do so many stupid things.

MICHAEL: *[short pause]* Gabriel?

GABRIEL: Yeah, Michael?

MICHAEL: *[concerned]* Is there anything we should do?

GABRIEL: No, we better wait for orders from God.

VOICE: Michael! Gabriel!

GABRIEL: I knew He'd come through.

MICHAEL: Incredible timing.

GABRIEL: He's the best.

VOICE: I need the two of you to go to planet Earth and encourage my servant Job. Do whatever you can to let him know that I love him and have a wonderful plan for him . . . not to harm him, but give him a future and a hope.

MICHAEL: *[looking up]* We'll get right on it, Sir.

GABRIEL: You know, it sure is great to know that God really does care for the people he created.

MICHAEL: Come on, we have a lot of work to do.

[Both exit as lights dim and music plays them off.]

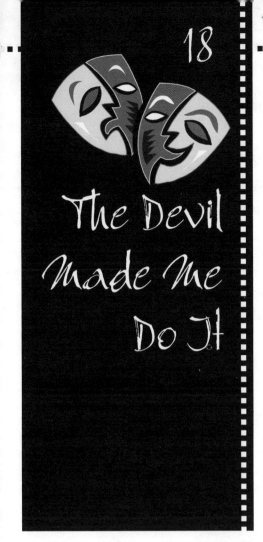

18

The Devil Made Me Do It

THEME

When we find ourselves in the predicaments of sinful choices, we love to blame the Devil. Since the Garden of Eden, temptation by the Devil has been the most common excuse in the book for sin. But we find these excuses run very short when challenged with the truth of our sinful desires and choices.

CHARACTERS

FRED FREEMAN: A good-natured sort of gent with casual attire and personality.

BILL WILLIAMS: A voice from within the box.

SETTING

At stage center is a chair or bench or couch. Next to the chair is a box on a small table or sitting on the floor.

Director's Note: Either name could be changed to a female person.

Fred enters, carrying a newspaper to sit in the chair or bench. He is happy-go-lucky with a lot of energy, singing or whistling as he walks onstage, sits, and reads out loud some headlines.

BILL: *[from the box, rather cordial]* Hey, would you mind keeping the noise down a bit?

FRED: *[Fred puts the paper down and looks around. He sees no one and continues reading the headlines.]*

BILL: *[louder]* Hey, buddy, do you mind?

FRED: *[responds more abruptly]* Okay . . . who said that?

BILL: I did.

FRED: *[looking all over and under his seat]* You did? Okay! Who are you and where are you?

BILL: Over here in the box. *[Fred looks the opposite way.]* No, over here, the other side . . . down . . . in . . . the . . . . box.

77

FRED: *[totally confused]* Wait a minute. You . . . whoever you are . . . you're in that box?

BILL: *[upset]* You got it, pal. So would you mind giving me some peace and quiet? I don't appreciate the noise.

FRED: *[concerned, with unbelief]* I don't know who you are, but *how* did you get in that box?

BILL: *[casually]* The Devil put me in here.

FRED: *[amazed]* The . . . Devil . . . put you in . . . there?

BILL: *[casually]* I think that's what I said.

FRED: But, *what* are you doing in that box?

BILL: *[factually speaking]* Sinning.

FRED: Sinning?

BILL: Yeah, sinning.

FRED: *[dumbfounded]* Sinning?

BILL: You have trouble hearing things, don't you?

FRED: *[baffled]* Why are you in there sinning?

BILL: The Devil makes me do it.

FRED: But what kind of sin can you do in that box?

BILL: What? You need a list? You don't get out much, do you, pal?

FRED: I just never met anyone sinning in a box before.

BILL: *[resolved]* Well, join the club. This wasn't my idea.

FRED: So why don't you get out?

BILL: The Devil won't let me.

FRED: *[more confused]* The Devil has you stuck in that box?

BILL: *[matter-of-factly]* Stuck as stuck can be.

FRED: *[trying to make sense]* Let me see if I have this straight. The Devil put you in that box. The Devil makes you sin inside that box. And the Devil won't let you get out.

BILL: *[excited]* Hey, you really do listen!

FRED: I just never heard of anything so ridiculous in all my life.

BILL: Hey, what's your name?

FRED: Fred, Fred Freeman, and who are you?

BILL: Bill, Bill Williams. I'd shake hands but the Devil won't let me out to do it.

FRED: *[serious]* Bill, how come the Devil has so much power over you?

BILL: Good question. But, Fred, let me ask you a question. Do you live in a house?

FRED: Well, sure I do.

BILL: Do you work in a building somewhere?

FRED: Yes, as a matter of fact I do.

BILL: So did you ever sin at work or at home and feel like you couldn't stop sinning?

FRED: *[embarrassed]* Well, as a matter of fact . . . I . . .

BILL: See, Fred, you're no different than me. My box is just smaller than your boxes.

FRED: But I don't give the Devil all the credit for making me sin. Those sins are all my personal choices.

BILL: *[celebrative]* Good for you, Fred. Thanks for being honest. At least I have an excuse. *[Fred looks puzzled.]*

[freeze; blackout; Music plays.]

19

Dear God, I Hate Pain

THEME

Everyone hates pain. Sometimes we tend to blame God for all the pain that is in our broken world. And when we do, it changes our whole perspective on what God wants to accomplish in our lives, as we will see in this sketch.

CHARACTERS

MORGAN: A woman of any age. She is dressed casually.

LINDSAY: Morgan's good friend, also dressed casually.

SETTING

At stage center is a small writing table and chair.

Morgan enters, carrying stationery and a pen. She sits and contemplatively begins to write.

MORGAN: *[thinking and talking]* Dear God . . . no. . . . To whom it may concern . . . no. . . . Dear Pain Maker. That's it. *[begins to write]* Dear Pain Maker. This letter is long overdue for all of the hurt and pain that You have caused me and my family. I hope You are happy that all of us are suffering. If this is some sort of sick cosmic joke, or some kind of heavenly humor, You need to know that none of us are laughing. So many times we asked You to take the hurt away, and we got more pain. We read Your Book and found others in pain and a few miracles that are only stories from ancient history. So, thank You, but no thank You for Your advice. You have been of no help to me or my family.

LINDSAY: *[coming around the corner]* Hello, is anybody home?

MORGAN: Hello, Lindsay, I'm over here.

LINDSAY: *[Lindsay walks over with great enthusiasm.]* Morgan, I've got two tickets for the big Annual Women's Glitz and Glitter Conference at the MegaDome. All your favorite singers and authors will be there. . . . It's sponsored by our church.

MORGAN: *[looking over her letter]* No thanks, Lindsay.

LINDSAY: *[shocked]* No thanks?

MORGAN: Yeah, no thanks!

LINDSAY: But, Morgan, you and I have attended the "Mega-Christian" event every year for the past eleven years, and you're saying, "No thanks?" What's up, girl?

MORGAN: *[dejected]* Just not interested, okay?

LINDSAY: *[selling the idea]* But Betty Lou Smiley is going to do her ventriloquism act, and Susanne Winter is going to tell us how to lose a few . . . you know . . . and Barbara Songland is going to sing from her new album. *[amazed]* You love these people, and all you can say is "No thanks."

MORGAN: Look, Lindsay, they're just going to prance onstage and say the same old things they always say. *[dramatically]* God is great and God is good.

LINDSAY: *[convinced]* But God is great and God is good.

MORGAN: Maybe to *you* He is.

LINDSAY: Morgan, what am I missing here?

MORGAN: I don't know, but I'm missing this year's "Glitz and Glitter."

LINDSAY: Is this about your sister?

MORGAN: Nope.

LINDSAY: Is this about Adam's cancer?

MORGAN: Nope.

LINDSAY: Okay, I got it. This is all about your dad losing his job and filing for bankruptcy. . . . Morgan, that was two years ago. Your family has got to move on.

MORGAN: *[getting harder]* Wrong again, best friend.

LINDSAY: So, what's this all about?

MORGAN: *[very definitive]* God!

LINDSAY: *[surprised]* God?

MORGAN: Yes, God . . . if there is one. Would you like to hear my letter to God?

LINDSAY: *[awkward and hesitant]* I'm not sure.

MORGAN: *[holding up letter]* If God is so great and so good, why all of the pain and hurt that my family has gone through this year?

LINDSAY: Well, maybe there is . . . or has been . . . or you know, not you, of course, but maybe . . . someone in your family has . . .

MORGAN: Sinned! Is that what you're trying to say?

LINDSAY: *[offended]* Well, that's a little harsh.

MORGAN: So this is all our fault and God is off the hook?

LINDSAY: *[really scrambling]* Well, not really. Maybe He just wants you to . . . get . . . become . . .

MORGAN: *[cynical]* Closer to God? Thanks for that number two answer. And if I get any closer, you're going to start calling me Mrs. God. *[very upset]* Try again, Pain Reliever.

LINDSAY: *[confused]* You know you're not making this very easy.

MORGAN: That's an understatement. And when was pain easy?

LINDSAY: Morgan, I know you've been through a lot and I'm sure that God is going to . . . you know, have some very special—

MORGAN: Blessings? Look, if God is looking for glory in all of this, He's going to have to change the program real fast. Nobody in our family is yelling any hallelujahs!!!

LINDSAY: *[pause, rips up brochure, and responds with warm sincerity]* How would you like to go for a long ride. I know a great place we can talk . . . and maybe pray.

[freeze; blackout]

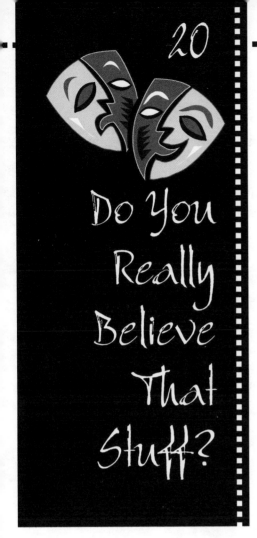

20

Do You Really Believe That Stuff?

THEME

Not everyone believes the stories or the truths of the Bible. Even believers struggle with what they believe to be true. In this sketch our Bible reader is challenged to defend her faith. She finds it is not easy.

CHARACTERS

SHARON: A Christian, dressed casually. She has her lunch bag, coke, and her Bible.

NANCY: Not a Christian. Dressed casually, she enters with a soda and piece of fruit.

SETTING

Two or three chairs and a folding table represent a lunchroom in any workplace.

As the music plays, Sharon enters, carrying her Bible under her arm and her lunch bag. She sits down, and after she takes out her sandwich, she looks about to make sure that nobody else is around. Then she opens her Bible and begins to read.

SHARON: *[Out loud, she begins reading her Bible then trails off.]* "Then the Lord said to Moses, what is that in your hand? Take your staff and throw it to the ground, and it became a snake." *[Sharon looks up with disgust.]* Ooo, I don't like snakes, I'm trying somewhere else. *[flips through her Bible]* "Better to live in a desert than with a quarrelsome and ill-tempered wife." *[looks up]* God, You just haven't met my husband, have You?

NANCY: *[walking in]* Hey, Sharon, what are you reading?

SHARON: *[embarrassed]* Oh, nothing . . . *[trying to hide the Bible]* . . . Just catching up on . . . you know, some old stories, novels . . . yeah, novels . . . just a few I wanted to check out.

NANCY: *[persistent and nosey, reaching over to the Bible and pulling it away, then as if horrified . . .]* Hey, this is a Bible.

SHARON: *[acting surprised]* Well, how about that, it sure is a Bible.

NANCY: [shocked] You're sitting here reading the Bible?

SHARON: [trying to come up with a fast excuse] Well, it was just lying here. Someone must have left it.

NANCY: [reads from the front] "To my daughter Sharon on her sixteenth birthday." Now, isn't that sweet? [teasing a little] There must be two Sharons that work here.

SHARON: [trying to act surprised] Oh my, what a coincidence.

NANCY: [serious] Now, tell me Sharon, do you believe the stuff you read in here?

SHARON: [sheepish] Well, I've always believed in the Bible and God and—

NANCY: [pushing a little] No, I mean, like the Flood and . . . the ark . . . and Mary being a virgin and all that stuff. Come on, do you really buy into all of that fairy-tale stuff?

SHARON: [tentative] Yeah, I guess I do.

NANCY: [direct] Can you prove any of those stories?

SHARON: [apprehensive] Well, not exactly.

NANCY: [being honest and sincere] So why bother?

SHARON: [thinking as she speaks] Well, I've always read from the Bible and my mom used to read the Bible and . . . you know, it is called the Good Book.

NANCY: [negative] I don't find anything good about plagues, floods, animal sacrifice, and hanging people on crosses.

SHARON: [thinking] You have a point.

NANCY: When you think about it, there aren't a lot of good stories in there. . . . [rather worked up] With all of the sex and violence in here, the book ought to be rated.

SHARON: [considering comment] You have a point.

NANCY: As a kid, the only thing I remember hearing was how sinful we are and how we'll pay big time in the end. [flipping through Bible]

SHARON: [forlorn] You have a point.

NANCY: Be honest, Sharon. Can you get your mind around all of this God talk?

SHARON: [agreeing] Well, you have a point.

NANCY: I mean listen to this, *[starts reading]* "For God so loved the world that he gave his only Son, that whoever believes in him will not die, but have everlasting life." Now, does that seem reasonable to you?

SHARON: *[sadly agreeing]* You *do* have a point.

NANCY: I mean who in the world would give up his only son for a bunch of people like us, and then tell the whole world by writing it down in a book?

SHARON: *[thinking for a moment, then sincere]* I think God would.

[freeze; blackout]

THEME

The true meaning of Christmas is lost in the busyness and materialism of our culture. A simple manger scene and a "talking shepherd" reminds us of who we should be focusing our attention upon during the Christmas—and every—season.

CHARACTERS

MR. DIRECTOR: A flamboyant Christmas-program director is hurrying to his performance. He hurries right past the manger scene, oblivious to the Christmas story.

MRS. SHOPALL: A fast-moving character, who is on a mission with her shopping bag and list. She is annoyed by the shepherd, who is trying to get her attention.

TEEN 1 and TEEN 2: Two young teen women are caught up in conversation about everything but the Christmas story. Their focus and attention is on the latest style and competition with friends.

BUSINESSMAN: Well-dressed, fast-moving business executive in full business suit, topcoat, and hat, carrying a cell phone.

YOUNG MAN: A young adult man appears quiet and forlorn. He's the only one who really listens to the shepherd.

SHEPHERD: Our talking shepherd is a voice offstage.

SETTING

A manger scene (crèche) is placed stage center on a small pedestal. A park bench is alongside the scene. Plenty of room should be allowed for characters to walk in front of the manger.

Director's Note: The following scenes can happen with or without a break between characters arriving on the platform.

INTRODUCTION

A Christmas carol is played while a "stagehand," wearing a headset or Walkman, enters, carrying the manger scene, and places it on the pedestal. The shepherd speaks the following as a voice-over to the music. Ideally, the houselights should go out with just a spot on the manger scene during the following monologue only, then the houselights should come up.

SHEPHERD: Hey, go easy with the setup, pal. Last year I fell out of this stable, and it was not a pretty sight. *[louder]* Hey, I'm talking to you. . . . I'm just asking you to be a little more careful . . . in case you forgot, we do have a baby in here. *[The stagehand is not sure what is happening as he looks around, then the shepherd speaks matter-of-factly.]* Look, folks, it wasn't my idea to be here. I was just minding my own business . . . taking care of my uncle's sheep, and now I have to do this manger scene thing every year. *[Music underscore begins.]* All I'm asking for is a few minutes to tell my story . . . or better yet, this little baby's story. . . . But I can see it's going to be another one of those years. So if you have a few minutes afterward, why not stop by. I'd love to chat with you. *[Music crescendos and lights go off.]*

SCENE 1

While a Christmas carol is played on a keyboard or tape, Mr. Director comes through the audience, complaining about being late for the performance. He's very dramatic as he spouts out the following, while walking across the stage toward the manger scene.

MR. DIRECTOR: Oh, I'm going to be late. What will the church do without me, the director of the Christmas pageant? There's so much to do. I'm sure everyone is in a panic. Why, the little lambs and the angels and shepherds will never make it without me. After all, I'm the most important person at this Christmas season.

SHEPHERD: *[as the director approaches the manger scene]* Ah, excuse me. . . . Hello . . . Mr. Christmas Pageant Director. . . . Hey, I'm down here. . . . Could I have about thirty seconds of your time?

MR. DIRECTOR: *[curious]* What's going on?

SHEPHERD: Okay . . . I promise to not take more than twenty seconds.

MR. DIRECTOR: *[melodramatic as he keeps moving]* I'm working too hard; I'm starting to hear things.

SHEPHERD: Hey, slow down and . . . *[after Mr. Director is past]* See what I mean, folks? Nobody has time to stop and talk. *[Music picks back up.]*

SCENE 2

Mrs. Shopall enters from the audience, carrying her bags, list, and so forth. She is also in a frantic hurry, trying to get everything done in time for Christmas. She's just as wired as Mr. Director.

MRS. SHOPALL: Oh, I have so much to do. . . . Now, where was that sale. . . . I know I have that five-cent coupon. . . . Mr. Shopall is going to have my head for spending too much. *[mumbling]* Now, let's see . . . last year I spent seven dollars on Alice, so I better . . . I just don't know how I'm going to do it all. *[holding up her cards or wallet, she proclaims]* I sure am glad God created credit cards. . . . I'll never leave home without these little wonders.

SHEPHERD: Excuse me, shopping lady. I have something I'd like to share with you. . . . It will only take a minute of your time.

MRS. SHOPALL: Who said that? I must be hearing things. . . . I must be going crazy.

SHEPHERD: Hey, lady, I have some really *good news* for you.

MRS. SHOPALL: I don't know who's saying that, but the only *good news* I'd like to hear is, "Attention shoppers there's a Blue Light special in aisle seven by the toy department." *[she scurries offstage]*

SHEPHERD: And there goes another. . . . If you folks know how I could get someone's attention to hear some good news, I sure would appreciate it. *[Music plays and lights fade out.]*

SCENE 3

As music plays, two teenage girls walk onstage, chatting about everything, and nothing. They are totally engaged in what they are sharing with each other.

TEEN 1: *[excited]* Did you see that guy parking the Jeep in the lot?

TEEN 2: *[dramatic]* You mean the one who looks like he stepped out of *GQ*?

TEEN 1: How come we never meet guys that look like that?

TEEN 2: Hey, what did you get your mom for Christmas?

TEEN 1: Nothing . . . yet. How about you?

TEEN 2: I bought my mom a new blow-dryer?

TEEN 1: Really? Is that what she wants for Christmas?

TEEN 2: No, but I need one, so why not . . . share . . . you know.

SHEPHERD: *[as the teens near the manger scene]* Hi, ladies. . . . Ah . . . do you have a minute?

TEEN 1: *[excited]* Did you hear a guy call us?

TEEN 2: *[shares the excitement]* Yeah, do you think it's the guy with the Jeep?

TEEN 1: Oh, my . . . how do I look? I knew I should have worn my Abercrombie sweater. . . .

SHEPHERD: *[as girls walk past the manger scene]* No, it's me, the shepherd from Bethlehem, not *GQ* . . . down here. I'm sorry I don't have a Jeep, and I don't care what kind of sweater you're wearing. . . . Really, it doesn't matter. Wow, to think the only good news this year is a four-wheel drive vehicle and some crummy sweater.

[Music plays and lights fade out.]

SCENE 4

Music continues as the businessman makes his way to the platform, talking on his cell phone. He is annoyed.

BUSINESSMAN: Look, Bill, can't you get anything right. *[more irritated as he speaks]* I told you that the Van Clydesdale account is a matter of life and death. We need to close on this before Christmas. . . . Four days left, Bill, count them, just four more days. My wife has charged so much money on Christmas gifts that I'm going to end up in the poorhouse. *[begins to yell]* I don't have *time* to listen to any excuses, I JUST WANT TO HEAR SOME *[yells louder]* GOOD NEWS!

SHEPHERD: *[excited]* Hey, Mr. Businessman, I have some good news.

BUSINESSMAN: *[Businessman spins around, looks at manger scene.]* What in the world . . .?

SHEPHERD: Sir, do you have a minute?

BUSINESSMAN: *[amazed he is talking to an inanimate object]* No, I don't have a minute. And what in the world am I talking to?

SHEPHERD: Just a simple old shepherd who spends a lot of time with baby Jesus.

BUSINESSMAN: *[throws his hands up in amazement]* I can't believe it—a talking manger scene. What will they think of next to get people to buy that stuff. That's all anyone thinks about—money, money, money. *[hurries offstage]*

SHEPHERD: *[trying to win him back]* I'm sorry . . . this really isn't about money. In fact, I don't have any money, just a few sheep and . . . and the Christ of Bethlehem.

[Light fades with music softly playing—"Silent Night."]

SCENE 5

The young man walks onstage. He does not speak as he walks. He sits at the park bench and looks sad, while he looks around and then down toward the ground with his hands cupped in front of him.

SHEPHERD: *[music stops]* Hi, can I talk with you? *[Young man looks around, saying nothing.]* Down here. I'm the shepherd next to the baby. I'm sorry I don't have a Jeep or a sweater, but I do have good news for you.

YOUNG MAN: *[discouraged tone]* What could possibly be of good news today?

SHEPHERD: *[sympathetic]* Whoa, you've had a bad day, huh?

YOUNG MAN: The worst day of my life. *[still looking down into hands]*

SHEPHERD: Would you care to talk about it? I'm not going anywhere for a while.

YOUNG MAN: *[holds a small ring in his hand]* Do you see this ring? I had everything riding on this stupid ring. I really love her. I love Jenny . . . but I guess she doesn't love me any more. At least that's what her note said.

SHEPHERD: Hey, I'm really sorry about you and Jenny.

YOUNG MAN: *[upset and hurt]* You know, she didn't even have the decency to call me on the phone. She just sends a card with my . . . her . . . ring in it. It really hurts, man; it really hurts. *[looks into manger scene]* But I guess I can't expect someone like you to understand.

SHEPHERD: I can see you're really hurting. And you're right, I can't understand what you're feeling. But I'd sure like to introduce you to someone who does know what you are feeling and really cares. So if you have a few minutes . . .

YOUNG MAN: Sure, why not. *[Music, "Silent Night," begins to softly play and lights begin to dim.]* I've got nothing more to lose.

[Music continues as someone leads the audience in singing "Silent Night" while man walks offstage.]